HIGHER EDUCATION ON THE MOVE:
NEW DEVELOPMENTS IN
GLOBAL MOBILITY

HIGHER EDUCATION ON THE MOVE: NEW DEVELOPMENTS IN GLOBAL MOBILITY

EDITED BY RAJIKA BHANDARI AND SHEPHERD LAUGHLIN

Second in a series of Global Education Research Reports

New York

IIE publications can be purchased at: www.iiebooks.org

The Institute of International Education
809 United Nations Plaza, New York, New York 10017

Library of Congress Cataloging-in-Publication Data

Higher education on the move : new developments in global mobility /
edited by Rajika Bhandari and Shepherd Laughlin.
        p. cm. -- (Global education research reports)
. Includes bibliographical references.
   ISBN 978-0-87206-315-0 (alk. paper)
  1. College teacher mobility. 2. College student mobility. 3.
International education. 4. Education and globalization. I. Bhandari,
Rajika. II. Laughlin, Shepherd, 1984- III. Institute of International
Education (New York, N.Y.)
  LB2335.3.H54 2009
  378'.016--dc22
                                    2009009194

TABLE OF CONTENTS

Series editors:
Daniel Obst, Director of Membership and Higher Education Services, IIE
Sharon Witherell, Director of Public Affairs, IIE

Cover image courtesy of Pierogi.
Ryan Mrozowski, "Drawing School," 2007. Acrylic on panel, 17 x 17 inches.
Collection of Susan Swenson and Joe Amrhein

In my paintings I depict crowds of figures gathered in the pursuit of knowledge and enter-tainment. My work is about the effort to understand our world through the various lenses of history, spirituality, science, music, horror films, consumerism, video games, theater productions, sports, literature, etc.
     —Ryan Mrozowski; studied British watercolor in Oxford, England

Cover and text design: Pat Scully Design

FIGURES AND TABLES

Figures

Tables

FOREWORD

By Allan E. Goodman
Institute of International Education

Today, about 3 million students and scholars are pursuing degrees and conducting research in a culture beyond their own—incredible, when we consider that until the 1930s, total worldwide higher education enrollment included less than 3 million students. Within the coming decade, the number of internationally mobile students and scholars will grow to 7 million and perhaps even reach 10 million.

There are at least four meanings attached to the concept of "international education." One is the current concept of globalization, which often refers to a sense that we should all be teaching and learning differently, in a way that recognizes that knowledge exists and is being created in cultures beyond our own.

A second meaning relates to phenomenon of branch campuses, which has been growing in scope and visibility during this decade, although there are still relatively small numbers of such campuses. In the 1970s Northeast Asia was the epicenter of this enterprise, while today it is the Arabian Gulf. I see a third use of the term "international education" in connection with the changing mission statements of colleges and universities, and even whole countries, that aspire to be world-class institutions of higher education and hubs at the center of learning.

The fourth definition is academic mobility, which is the subject of this book. It focuses attention on the trends and dynamics driving the circulation of students and scholars across national boundaries. At the Institute, we capture this in our annual *Open Doors* survey, which reports the numbers of international students and scholars in America and Americans studying abroad, and with *Project Atlas*, which looks at these flows on a global basis.

The challenge to each higher education institution is to answer the questions of who, what, where, when, and how such mobility can best be promoted and why, fundamentally, it is desirable. The essays here all aim to inform discussion as an increasing number of colleges and universities are making international a more central part of what it means to be educated.

Allan E. Goodman
President & CEO, Institute of International Education

By William L. Gertz
American Institute for Foreign Study

Any discussion related to global student mobility must be seen in the context of the current worldwide financial crisis.

While it is quite clear that students have the desire to be educated abroad and that educators and administrators are working hard to eliminate a wide variety of barriers (e.g., credit transfer, university calendars, course offerings), it is also apparent that financial considerations will be the number one factor limiting student mobility. For example, last year some 150,000 South Korean students went abroad for some kind of study. This year, that number is likely to fall by 30 to 40 percent, according to a recent article in the New York Times. Reductions in other countries are sure to follow, reversing a decade-long trend of increases.

That said, we believe there is much momentum building which will enable student mobility to increase after the downturn ends. Long-term mobility trends are extremely positive—the British Council, in its own Vision 2020 Forecast on International Student Mobility (published in 2004), reported that global demand for international higher education student placements will increase from 2.1 million students in 2003 to 5.8 million students in 2020.

National governments and private sector organizations will play a role in building a globally educated generation, but it is the students themselves who will make student mobility a reality. According to Mark Kopenski, Vice President and Dean of Enrollment for Richmond, The American International University in London which enrolls nearly 1100 students from across the globe, "Students want to consume education in a variety of ways delivered in traditional and nontraditional methods (podcasts for example) when they want to consume it. They want to be portable—take courses in Boston, London, Dubai and Beijing, do it seamlessly and obtain a degree that will get them a management job as quickly as possible."

The essays in this book outline some of the challenges and possibilities and present new research in student mobility in higher education. Many thanks to the authors for their critical thinking and fresh view points.

William L. Gertz
President & CEO, American Institute For Foreign Study
Trustee, American Institute For Foreign Study Foundation

INTRODUCTION

BY RAJIKA BHANDARI
DIRECTOR OF RESEARCH AND EVALUATION
INSTITUTE OF INTERNATIONAL EDUCATION, NEW YORK

Back in 1992, when I arrived in the United States as an international student from India, the world was a very different place for the 1.3 million hopefuls who had chosen to leave the shores of their home country to further their higher education in a foreign land. For one, the internet and email—the very lifelines of internationalization, some would argue—were still in their infancy. The process of becoming a globally mobile student was fairly straightforward, and the accompanying choices limited to information that was easily available through surface mail and the overseas outposts of popular higher education destinations. For me, and for most others in my cohort, the obvious choice was either the UK or the U.S.—Australia had not become the serious contender that it is today, and language was still a barrier in continental Europe. Information was gathered by visiting EducationUSA advising centers to peruse hardcopy catalogues and brochures of various U.S. universities and colleges seeking to attract international students. There were no slickly designed websites dedicated to the institution's internationalization efforts.

But the sheer availability of information for today's international student is not the only change that has taken place. International students of my generation typically pursued a traditional path: a highly structured course of study or degree obtained at an overseas institution in a major Anglophone country. We could never have imagined a future where we could get the best of both worlds: courses taken simultaneously in two different countries and as part of two different education systems—what are today known as dual or joint degrees; that a handful of countries in the West were not the only option for a top-notch education; and that places like China, Singapore, and Qatar would become sought-after educational destinations. And finally, who would have believed that obtaining a degree from an overseas institution would be possible without ever leaving the physical boundaries of one's country—a development that is made possible by today's off-shore education and branch campuses.

In essence, what we understand as global higher education mobility today has changed dramatically in the past several years alone. Today's international student is a savvy consumer, making well-informed choices and seeking a top-quality education regardless of geographic, language, or curricular boundaries. But students are not the only drivers of mobility and internationalization. Higher education institutions, on their part, have positioned themselves to meet the demands of an increasingly competitive higher education "marketplace" and the needs of their 2.9 million bright and talented consumers. Teaching and research faculty are travelling across the globe—in real and virtual time—bringing back to their classrooms, campuses, and disciplines a wealth of culturally nuanced knowledge.

The Institute has a long history of researching critical developments in global higher education mobility. In this report, the second in a series of Global Education Research Reports produced by IIE and the AIFS Foundation, we explore the rapid growth of the scale and nature of mobility, while focusing on specific developments and strategies world-wide that have contributed to this expansion. Our contributors for this volume were selected carefully to represent a diversity of expertise, world regions and perspectives. While most belong to the field of international education, others, such as Galama and Hosek from the RAND Corporation, bring a different and valuable perspective to mobility issues. The wide perspectives of our authors are also evident in occasional variations in comparable data cited in their chapters—reminding us that there is no single definition or approach to measuring and reporting mobility-related statistics.

Our report opens with two chapters that lay the groundwork for those that follow. In Chapter 1, Rajika Bhandari and Peggy Blumenthal provide an overview of current global mobility issues, while also focusing on evolving definitions of mobility and the measurement of this phenomenon through efforts such as Project Atlas. Chapter 2, by N. V. Varghese, addresses the overarching issue that in an era of mounting global competitiveness, higher education is no longer viewed as just a social good but is in fact considered to be a market-driven activity. The chapter takes a look at the GATS trade agreements that have significant implications for higher education mobility. Building upon the brief discussion of faculty mobility in Chapter 2, Sabine O'Hara devotes Chapter 3 to exploring a critical aspect of mobility—the movement of scholars across borders and the impact of this mobility on the generation of knowledge, pedagogy, and research.

The next set of chapters looks at critical developments in Europe that have implications not only for intra-Europe mobility, but also for student and scholar mobility between Europe and other countries. In Chapter 4, Bernd Wächter examines the impact of the European Bologna Process on the mobility of students. Drawing upon their experiences at the University of Graz in Austria, Roberta Maierhofer and Ulla Kriebernegg explore in Chapter 5 the relatively new frontier of joint and dual degree programs in international higher education, and the opportunities and challenges inherent in developing and administering these sorts of innovative ventures.

In Chapter 6, Ellen Hazelkorn emphasizes the role global university rankings play in a highly competitive higher education marketplace where international students often base their selection of an institution on ranks and metrics, and where institutions use rankings as a way to compete for global talent. Chapter 7 by Titus Galama and James Hosek also addresses the issue of global competition, but from the perspective of science and technology and the role of mobility in ensuring competitiveness in a knowledge economy.

Global higher education mobility—whether undertaken by students, scholars or institutions—is expanding rapidly and, like any other burgeoning phenomenon, is likely to have some unintended consequences. We conclude our report with Chapter 8, in which Jane Knight advises all those in the business of international education to proceed with cautious optimism. She reminds us that although internationalization in all its forms has been largely beneficial and positive, there are some drawbacks that require careful scrutiny and regulation by nations and higher education systems.

We are delighted to bring you this multifaceted exploration of global mobility issues and hope that you will find this report to be useful and informative.

Chapter One

GLOBAL STUDENT MOBILITY: MOVING TOWARDS BRAIN EXCHANGE*

BY RAJIKA BHANDARI AND PEGGY BLUMENTHAL,

INSTITUTE OF INTERNATIONAL EDUCATION

Global higher education mobility is a rapidly growing phenomenon with over 2.9 million students seeking an education outside their home country.[1] This number represents a 57 percent increase since 1999 and the greatest surge in international student enrollments in recent decades. But although the rapid growth of mobility is relatively recent, the desire to acquire a higher education beyond national borders is itself not new: students and scholars have always sought learning at the best higher education institutions around the world as a way to broaden their educational and cultural horizons. The Renaissance Dutch scholar Erasmus, after whom the first European Union (EU) mobility schemes were named, embodied the tradition of travel and study which existed in Europe at the time, as well as in Asia and the Middle East. More recently, not only has the number of internationally mobile students grown, but the overall context of global mobility—both in terms of who is going where, and the mix of host and sending countries—has also changed significantly. Most countries now view international academic mobility and educational exchanges as critical components for sharing knowledge, building intellectual capital and remaining competitive in a globalizing world.

The rising number of mobile students is perhaps partly an outcome of the worldwide growth in higher education. Globally, domestic higher education enrollment in 2005 increased to 144 million students, up from 68 million in 1991, with countries in Asia and the Pacific seeing the largest growth.[2] Some rapidly growing Asian countries such as Malaysia and China have recently almost doubled their higher education enrollments. At the same time, these burgeoning higher education populations have put enormous pressure on the higher education systems of many developing countries, especially at the post-graduate level, leading large numbers of their students to seek higher education outside of their home country. India is one such example where the growth of the college-age population has outpaced the capacity of the country's existing higher education institutions. There remains, thus, an enormous unmet and growing demand for international education and a huge capacity worldwide to absorb more international students.

---

* A previous version of this chapter appeared in the *The Europa World of Learning 2008, 1*. London: Routledge.

In this chapter we examine current trends in international mobility and explore factors that contribute to these trends. In doing so, we draw upon the Institute of International Education's (IIE) extensive research in this area, as well as research conducted by other experts who have examined this issue from a variety of angles. The chapter begins by addressing the issue of how to define and measure global student mobility, as this lays the groundwork for discussing trends and variations in global mobility patterns. Next, we examine some key developments that have contributed to the shifting picture of global mobility. Having explored the current status and drivers of mobility trends, we conclude the chapter by examining the implications of these trends at the national and institutional levels. In doing so, we expand our focus beyond higher education to include skilled employment because the two are inextricable and critical components of the education-to-employment pipeline in countries that attract international students and skilled migrants.

Who is an International Student? The Challenges of Measuring Global Mobility

Which are the largest sending and host countries? Where do the students come from and where do they go? Attempting to answer these critical questions, many countries have established their own systems for collecting information on international students. In the U.S., for example, IIE has been collecting this type of data since the 1920s and has published it as the *Open Doors Report on International Educational Exchange* since 1954, with support from the U.S. Department of State since 1972.[3] An annual census of U.S. international educational exchange, *Open Doors* presents mobility statistics based on data collected from all regionally accredited U.S. higher education institutions. Similar data for Australia are gathered by Australian Education International (AEI), for the UK by the Higher Education Statistics Agency, and for Germany by the German Academic Exchange Service (DAAD). Countries such as China (through the China Scholarship Council, CSC) and Mexico (through the Association of Universities and Higher Education Institutions, ANUIES) have more recently developed mechanisms to collect this type of data.

But country-specific data by themselves are limited in that they tell us little about the implications of each country's mobility statistics within a global context. Although global mobility involves over 2.9 million students, the worldwide data on this phenomenon are limited and imperfect. Transnational comparisons can be problematic because different countries use different data definitions and time frames. The variation in national degree and qualifications structures across countries also makes comparative analysis difficult.

While UNESCO and OECD have instituted large-scale efforts to collect mobility data for all countries, they face a number of limitations. For one, there is typically a time lag between the year the data are collected and released. Second, because the data are primarily collected through ministries of education, they do not always capture enrollments at private institutions. The result is an underestimate of international students, since private institutions represent the fastest growing education sector in many countries. Third, according to the definitions used by UNESCO and OECD, only students enrolled for the duration of a year or more are counted in the data. Since internationally mobile students from the U.S., Japan and the EU often study abroad for less than a full academic year, it can be safely assumed that the actual number of students who are globally mobile might significantly exceed the 2.9 million reported by OECD.

One effort to build upon the work of UNESCO and OECD and address some of its limitations is *Project Atlas*, a Ford Foundation-supported program that is building a community of researchers from around the world to share more current and direct data on student mobility.[4] *Project Atlas* provides a comprehensive global picture of international student mobility for 27 leading destination countries and enrollment by students from 75 places of origin. Current project partners include ANUIES, the Association of Indian Universities (AIU), AEI, British Council, the CSC, DAAD, the International Education Association of South Africa (IEASA), and the Netherlands Organization for International Cooperation in Higher Education (NUFFIC), among others. The project allows researchers, policymakers, and other stakeholders to situate mobility trends within a global context and to understand their implications for higher education and the labor market. Another key feature of the project is that it allows users to examine international education patterns in relation to other national developments such as home country investment in human capital, population growth, and the expansion of technological capacity.

While Anglophone and Western European countries such as the U.S., the UK, Australia, France, and Germany have historically attracted the largest number of international students, other countries have boosted their internationalization strategies in recent years to attract more students, build university linkages, and develop joint research programs. In an effort to illuminate the national policies that facilitate global mobility, *Atlas* partner organizations use the project website to share the strategies and initiatives their countries and governments have undertaken to increase international educational exchange. To capture more fully the increasingly important role that newer host countries are now playing in global mobility, an ongoing challenge for *Project Atlas* is to identify and involve more partners from Asia, Latin America, the Middle East, and Africa.

Current Trends: Who is Going Where?

Many factors, real or perceived, can affect a student's choice of study destination, including the cost and quality of higher education programs; the value of the degree or professional credential for future careers; the availability of certain areas of specialization; access to the education system and a country (including, but not limited to, obtaining visas for entry); and important historical, linguistic and geographic links between the home and destination country. Drawing upon statistical sources such as *Open Doors*, *Project Atlas*, and UNESCO and OECD data, this section presents key trends in global education mobility and also examines past and current projections of growth in this area.

At the turn of the millennium, several studies documented the rise in international student mobility and suggested that the numbers would inevitably increase. In a prominent report published in 2002, IDP Education Australia projected a dramatic expansion in the demand for international education, doubling over the next 10 years and then perhaps doubling again, with as many as 7.2 million students studying outside their home country by the year 2025 (Bohm, Davis, Meares, & Pearce, 2002). Seven years after these initial projections, it appears that these high estimates did not fully account for the rapid expansion of the higher education sector in countries such as China that have since gone beyond functioning primarily as sending countries to also become attractive host destinations, especially for students from within the region. For example, in just one year, international enrollment in Chinese universities has risen from 162,695 students in 2006 to195,503 in 2007/08, a 20 percent increase (*Project Atlas*, 2008). In a more recent forecasting study conducted in 2007, IDP has revised its calculations of student mobility growth and has now estimated a total of 3.7 million mobile students by 2025.

Despite the inherent limitations of their methodology, the estimates released by UNESCO and OECD have remained fairly stable over time. In 2000, UNESCO estimated that almost 2 million higher education students were being educated in countries other than their homes; current estimates indicate that approximately 2.9 million students (most from the developing world) are currently mobile, a large proportion of whom—45 percent—are in major Anglophone host countries, defined as Australia, Canada, the UK and the U.S. Students from the traditional destination countries in Europe and in the U.S. are also pursuing international education in increasing numbers. Data from *Open Doors* show that the number of American students studying abroad has more than quadrupled since the mid-1980s (Bhandari & Chow, 2008). Countries within the EU have experienced even greater expansion of their internationally mobile student populations due to EU-funded programs such as Erasmus, Socrates and Leonardo, as well as the structural reforms initiated through the Bologna Process. The EU estimates that 1.4 million European students have already participated in the Erasmus program.

Based on the data sources mentioned above, we summarize below some key trends that have emerged recently:

- Eight countries host 72 percent of the world's tertiary-level mobile students: the U.S. (20 percent), the UK (13 percent), Germany (8 percent), France (8 percent), Australia (7 percent), China (7 percent), Canada (5 percent) and Japan (4 percent). Anglophone countries such as Australia and the UK have seen large percentage increases in their international student populations, while the U.S. has seen a modest decline. However, the U.S. continues to host the largest number and proportion of international students pursuing a higher education outside of their home country (623,805 students in 2007/08), followed by the UK at 376,190 students in 2007 (*Project Atlas*, 2008). Looking at the rate of growth, the rate for the U.S. is understandably less than those of other countries that are starting out from a much smaller base: the U.S. has hosted over half a million students for the past eight years while Australia, for example, hosted 202,448 students in 2007, resulting in a steeper rate of increase.

- The overall pie of global mobility is expanding with more countries emerging as important destinations for international students. Newer host countries such as China are seeing rapid increases in the numbers of international students. Several other countries in the Asia Pacific region—Thailand, Malaysia, Singapore and New Zealand, to name a few—have stepped up their efforts to internationalize and to attract more international students. Even though this has resulted in a somewhat smaller market share for the U.S., we believe that this is a positive development as it has brought more countries into the field of international education and has changed the dynamic between sending and receiving countries from a unidirectional "brain drain" type of mobility to one of true mutual exchange.

- The largest groups of internationally mobile students come from East Asia and the Pacific (29 percent). Students from China represent the largest share of internationally mobile students (15 percent), followed by students from India, South Korea, Japan and Germany.

- In terms of world regions, sub-Saharan Africa has the highest outbound mobility share of its total higher education population (6 percent), almost three times greater than the world average. North America (U.S. and Canada) has the lowest outbound ratio with only 0.4 percent of the region's tertiary students pursuing their education abroad.

The Expanding Universe of Academic Mobility: Old and New Players

Developed countries in Europe, North America and Oceania have dominated the global mobility picture of the late 20th and early 21st century. The U.S., UK, France and Germany, in particular, have long attracted large numbers of international students. For the most part, the movement of students has been from developing to developed countries (Altbach, 2007; Altbach & Knight, 2007; UNESCO, 2006). And while this overall trend continues today, the situation is nonetheless changing for these key countries, with interesting variations emerging in which several unexpected players are now engaged in what might best be described as a "global competition" for international students. As a result, international students are not only choosing nontraditional destinations but are also pursuing nontraditional forms of learning.

These changes have been propelled by a combination of factors. These include the expanding capacity of countries like China to not only provide more higher education opportunities for their own students but to also host an increasing number of international students; the availability and global spread of alternative modes of educational delivery; and domestic economic, demographic, and workforce conditions that might affect students' decisions regarding an overseas education. For example, it is quite possible that reported declines in international students pursuing science and engineering degrees in the U.S. might have more to do with the growing value of degrees in business and management in key sending countries such as India and China and less to do with the presumed decline in America's appeal as a destination for studying science and engineering. In this section, we examine in detail four interrelated developments in international education that have contributed to a significant shift in the demand and supply equation of global mobility.

Increased Recruiting of International Students

Government-supported efforts by key host countries, including nationally coordinated campaigns by the UK, Australia, Germany, France, New Zealand and others, feature sophisticated marketing strategies and expedited visa policies. Several of these host countries, along with newer players in Asia and Europe, have allocated tens of millions of dollars to launch large-scale initiatives over the past few years. These efforts are proving very persuasive, especially to self-funded students from some of the large sending countries in Asia.

Launched in 1998, the UK's £5 million "Prime Minister's Initiative" was one of the earliest and was updated in 2000 as the "Education UK" brand, a coordinated approach to marketing British institutions abroad that is available for use by any UK campus. Other recent UK initiatives include the Science and Engineering Graduate Scheme (2004), the UK-China Higher Education Program (2005), and the UK-India Education and Research Initiative (2006).

Countries that were primarily "sending" countries have now also developed their own internationalization strategies to attract foreign students and encourage international educational exchange. Singapore has been making strides in this area with the establishment of Education Singapore, a new agency charged with promoting and marketing Singapore abroad and with attracting 150,000 foreign students by 2015. Malaysia seeks to attract 100,000 international students by 2010 (up from 45,000 in 2005); Jordan announced plans to increase the number of international students to 100,000 by 2020; China seeks to host 300,000 by 2020; and Japan has reportedly set the ambitious goal of hosting one million foreign students by 2025 (up from the current 120,000).[5]

Many countries are also formalizing the link between higher education and the skilled job market by implementing policies that encourage international graduates to enter the workforce of the host country, especially in scientific and technical fields. Scotland announced a "Post-Study Worker Scheme" aimed at attracting 8,000 foreign professionals per year up until 2009 by allowing international students who graduate from a Scottish university to remain for two years of post-graduation employment. Supplementing efforts by individual host countries in Europe, the EU has also launched initiatives to recruit science and technology researchers from around the world in an attempt to compete with America's well-funded research universities and labs that reputedly attract the world's best and brightest S&T talent.

Home Country Higher Education Capacity

In China, India, South Korea and many other countries, the number of higher education seats at home has grown dramatically as national and provincial/state governments increase their investments in public education. Within some countries, especially in Asia and Latin America, the private higher education sector is also dramatically expanding to meet growing demand. But despite the rapid expansion of the public and private education sector in many countries, it is worth noting that the burgeoning college-age population in China and India continues to exceed the domestic higher education capacity of these countries, a demand-supply imbalance that probably partly explains the growing numbers of Chinese and Indian students who continue to seek an overseas education.

Growth in Other Forms of "International Education"

A range of new institutions and alternative approaches to "international" study have emerged to meet the growing need for a cost-effective education, and as a result many students are choosing to stay home while also acquiring an "international" education (Blumenthal, 2002). These new modes of education include, among others, distance learning, joint degrees, branch campuses, and "sandwich" programs involving short-term study abroad. According to Gray (2006), these types of nontraditional academic arrangements have succeeded because they offer alternative modes of organization and operation in the form of new program offerings (e.g., short courses, night classes); new pedagogical approaches; asynchronous and collaborative learning; and distributed physical infrastructure including, but not limited to, remote campuses and distance education via the internet.

Perhaps the most significant development in alternative forms of international education has been the advent of the branch campus, often referred to as Trans-National Education (TNE), borderless education, or cross-border education. Broadly speaking, this approach involves "the movement of education across national jurisdictional or geographic borders" (Knight, 2006a)—that is, "internationalization abroad" as compared with the more traditional form of "internationalization at home" (IAU, 2006). As in the case of more traditional forms of global student mobility, the movement and spread of cross-border education has primarily been from the developed North to the developing South. U.S. institutions continue to dominate this type of overseas delivery and account for more than half of all overseas higher education, followed by Australia, the UK and Ireland (Verbik & Merkley, 2006). Key host countries for overseas campuses include Singapore and China in Asia, and Dubai (Knowledge Village) and Qatar (Education City) in the Middle East.

Cross-border education has significant implications for domestic and international higher education. It is conceivable, for example, that as prospective international students choose branch campuses located in their own countries over the institution's home campus, traditional student mobility, as we know it, might decline (Knight, 2006b). The expansion of "virtual mobility" through internet-based learning may also undercut the need for students to cross physical borders to obtain an international credential. Conversely, it is also possible that these diverse forms of internationalization will continue to grow rapidly, serving different types of students with varying educational needs.[6]

Nontraditional Mobility Patterns

Although there are no hard data to support this assertion, anecdotal evidence suggests that international mobility or skilled migration no longer follows a strictly linear pattern where people move between just two countries, typically from South to North. In an increasingly connected world, a student from Asia, for example, might choose to obtain an undergraduate degree in her home country, a master's degree in the U.S., and a doctoral degree in the UK, returning home subsequently to work for a European multinational firm. The mobility of international scientists and researchers, too, has become increasingly complex as the field of science and engineering itself has evolved into a borderless enterprise. Not surprisingly, this type of multicountry mobility is difficult to measure. For instance, even though Finn's (2007) groundbreaking research on the "stay rates" of international postdoctoral researchers and scholars in the U.S. sheds light on who remains in the U.S. and who leaves, it is not able to tell us whether those who leave are heading to another country or back to their home country, or even whether those staying on in the U.S. are commuting between the U.S. and their home country regularly to work in joint ventures.

The Brain Exchange: Implications of Global Mobility Trends

Although many researchers use the framework of "brain drain" and "brain gain" to analyze trends and outcomes of global mobility and skilled migration, this implies a unidirectional, linear approach to mobility that does not fully capture the current reality of international flows. Early assessments of skilled migration emphasized the "brain drain" aspect of such mobility, arguing that because mobility was primarily from the developing to the developed world, it resulted in a drain of the former's human resources; later interpretations of skilled migration rejected the inequitable aspect of mobility and suggested that the drain should be regarded as a "brain gain" situation whereby sending countries actually stand to benefit, primarily financially, from skilled migration.[7]

Like many others in the field, we employ the "brain" metaphor, while also offering a new and more nuanced interpretation of it that takes into account current mobility trends. We prefer the terms "brain circulation" or "brain exchange" to account for the increasingly multidirectional nature of mobility and the growing awareness that such mobility patterns or exchanges are mutually beneficial for sending and receiving countries, albeit in varying ways. It is important to mention, however, that the one major exception to this shift is Africa, as it continues to lose a disproportionate amount of its human resources to skilled migration. Coupled with the widespread destruction of human capital caused by the AIDS epidemic and repeated political upheavals, outward migration of talented individuals has taken a heavy toll on the continent's social, economic and educational sectors (Teferra, 2005).

While there is as yet limited empirical evidence in support of the circulation of global knowledge and talent, related trends and anecdotal reports present an interesting picture. Combining findings for the U.S. from Finn's stay rates analysis with data from *Open Doors 2008*, we find that two of the major sending places, South Korea and Taiwan, have fairly low stay rates in the U.S. (Bhandari & Chow, 2008; Finn, 2007). In other words, although large numbers of students from Taiwan and South Korea seek higher education in the U.S., a large proportion, many of whom might be scientists or engineers, are also likely to take their knowledge and skills back to their places of origin. However, this was not always the case. Taiwan's stay rates in the 1950s and 1960s rivaled India's today, but the rapid expansion of Taiwan's economy and political reforms of the 1980s and 1990s made opportunities at home more attractive to recent graduates of U.S. universities. We are seeing similar trends with Chinese graduates whose career opportunities in Shanghai or Singapore draw them back to Asia within a few years of graduating from institutions in the U.S. or the UK.

The strengthening of overseas higher education partnerships, facilitated by advances in telecommunications and the internet, have also contributed to the shift from a drain to a balance in the sharing of knowledge and information. For instance, faculty and researchers at foreign and U.S. universities have significantly increased their collaboration, and research activities now regularly span multiple countries while capitalizing on worldwide knowledge and talent (Adams, Black, Clemmons, & Stephan, 2004).

To take advantage of the global knowledge and skills required in a knowledge economy and to meet the demand for skilled labor, many countries have launched extensive efforts and initiatives to recruit scientists and engineers to return home. Returning skilled workers are seen as improving a country's productivity and global competitiveness because of the direct transfer of knowledge and skills and the indirect benefits that accrue through returnees' access to overseas professional and trade networks that can have positive impact on domestic growth and development (Thorn & Holm-Nielsen, 2006).

It is not surprising that places such as Singapore, South Korea and Taiwan—places that have well-developed industrial and science and technology sectors offering attractive opportunities and compensation for highly skilled professionals—are also the ones with the most successful return rates (Meyer & Brown, 1999). For example, Taiwan has focused its efforts on providing challenging opportunities for returning young researchers through the establishment of science-based industrial parks. Keeping in mind the higher standard of living in the developed countries in which its expatriate nationals typically reside, Malaysia used the strategy of providing tax exemptions to returning nationals to compensate for the potentially lower income (Lowell, 2001). Between 1991 and 2000, the Presidential Fund for Retention in Mexico successfully repatriated 2,000 overseas Mexican-born researchers at a total cost of US$56 million (NSF, 2000).

Some countries are also experimenting with the western model of competitive funding for research and innovation as a repatriation strategy (Thorn & Holm-Nielsen, 2006). The Chinese research system provides an interesting example. In an attempt to attract back its researchers and scientists, the Chinese government is shifting from a more Soviet-style centralized research system to one that provides competitive research grants through an impartial, peer-review process (Jonkers, 2004). According to one estimate, the number of returnees almost doubled between 2001 and 2002, reaching close to 18,000 in 2002 (Zweig, Changgui, & Rosen, 2004). A similar approach has been adopted in Chile, Brazil, Mexico, Venezuela and Vietnam through the Millennium Science Initiative, an international program designed to build capacity in modern science and engineering and examine their uses in developing countries.

One of the newest players in the Asian region is Pakistan. Launched in 2002, the Pakistani Higher Education Commission (HEC) is an umbrella organization vested with creating academic linkages between Pakistani higher education institutions and foreign universities through an initial investment of US$5 million (Atta-ur-Rahman, 2007). Among its key strategies to promote bidirectional exchange is the Foreign Faculty Hiring Program, which recruits highly qualified faculty members from abroad for both short- and long-term appointments. So far, over 270 faculty have participated in the program. Efforts to attract back highly skilled Pakistani migrants are complemented by the desire to provide more Pakistani students with the opportunity to obtain an international education and to reinvigorate their country's higher education sector with their newly acquired knowledge. To this end, close to 4,200 students are eligible for a variety of scholarships, including those available through the Fulbright program, that will enable them to acquire advanced research training overseas. Similar efforts are underway in Saudi Arabia, including the establishment of a multimillion dollar overseas scholarship fund and the creation in 2007 of a new world-class university intended to attract international graduate students in science and technology fields.[8]

Key Implications for Developed and Developing Countries

The emergence and growing popularity of alternative higher education destinations, coupled with increasing return rates for a few key "source" countries, leads to the inevitable question: can the perennial favorite hosts—most of which are large, developed countries—maintain their competitive edge by attracting the best and the brightest from around the world? For instance, the U.S.—which remains to date the top choice of international students and scholars—is affected the most by current trends in global student mobility and skilled migration. U.S. reliance on foreign-born talent grew in both absolute numbers and as a share of the science and engineering workforce during the 1990s (National Science Board, 2008). In 2005, foreign-born students earned 50 percent or more of U.S. doctoral degrees in mathematics, computer sciences, physics, engineering, and economics. The proportion of foreign-born faculty in the science, technology, engineering and mathematics (STEM) fields increased from 38 percent in 1992 to 47 percent in 2003 at U.S. research institutions.

The key challenge for countries like the U.S. that have come to rely on international talent is to strike the right balance between increasing domestic science and technology capacity while also attracting the best and the brightest from around the world. To view these strategies as mutually exclusive is to impose boundaries upon the science and innovation enterprise that, by its very nature, has become global and borderless. Keeping the doors open to international students and scholars, many of whom go on to become immigrants, also has multiplier effects: the children of immigrants show a very high interest in science and technology. According to the National Foundation of American Policy, 60 percent of top science students and 60 percent of top math students in U.S. high schools are children of immigrants (Anderson, 2004). A detailed study of engineering and technology companies started in the U.S. between 1995 and 2005 found that over a quarter were founded by immigrants (primarily Indians, followed by those from the UK, China, Taiwan, and Japan), employing 450,000 workers nationwide, and accounting for $52 billion in total sales (Wadhwa, Saxenian, Rissing & Gereffi, 2007).

But underlying the tension between creating opportunities for Americans while also attracting global talent is the issue—perhaps more fundamental—of the number of college graduates required to meet America's future workforce needs. In other words, is it just a matter of science and technology capacity or is there an overall shortage of highly skilled workers? According to a recent report released under the Making Opportunity Affordable Initiative (Lumina Foundation), there is a significant "degree gap" in the U.S. as compared with other leading developed nations, defined as the difference between degrees produced in the U.S. (relative to its laborforce needs) and those produced by nations that are top competitors (Reindl, 2007). At the current pace of production, the U.S. will produce about 41 million degrees by 2025, leaving a gap of 22 million between the country's laborforce needs and the actual availability of an adequate educated and skilled workforce. When adjusted for net gains from immigrants with degrees (that is, those entering the U.S. with postsecondary degrees minus degree-holders leaving the U.S.), the degree gap will amount to 16 million degrees.

Developing countries have traditionally been the "suppliers" of international students but now face interesting challenges as they also become hosts to international students. Developing countries that are poised to become popular study destinations are likely to face a dilemma: how to increase the capacity of their higher education systems to provide adequate opportunities for their expanding college-age population while also accommodating incoming international students and engaging in the type of international educational exchange that is necessary in today's globally competitive world. Last but not the least, a related challenge for developing countries hoping to attract back their nationals will be to ensure adequate employment opportunities and an appropriate standard of living.

Conclusion

The movement of students and scholars across borders is growing rapidly, driven by many factors, and involving a wide range of vehicles and modalities. There are a variety of objectives and approaches to engaging in academic exchange, and countries and institutions that are most effective in internationalizing are characterized by flexibility and a willingness to adapt to new realities in the complex world of higher education. Common to the best of them are certain elements such as commitment to academic excellence, to fair and open access for candidates, and to a diverse range of participants. Most also face similar challenges, such as how to cope with rapidly expanding opportunities and interest in study abroad with limited or shrinking resources.

Indeed, according to some estimates, the desire for higher education—and the subsequent demand for international education—is expanding so rapidly that in 20 years there will not be enough classroom seats in the whole world to meet the needs of students who want to pursue higher education. Creative and collaborative solutions will be needed to provide higher education and training to those who seek it. Distance learning, joint degree programs, and new approaches we cannot yet imagine will all be needed to address the educational needs of the hundreds of millions of undergraduates around the world. Governments will, of course, be the primary responders to this need, but the private and non-profit sectors are also likely to play key roles.

At the institutional level, many universities in a few countries are starting to develop branch campuses abroad, so that they can reach the billions of students who cannot afford to study abroad but who desire access to international education. These programs have their own challenges and need to be very responsive to the needs and requirements of the host country. They can never fully replace the kind of intense cultural learning experience of plunging into a foreign environment and mastering the linguistic and cultural and academic challenges of studying abroad. Thus, we see an important role for both kinds of "international education" and hope that they can reinforce each other in the coming decades.

Finally, we cannot ignore the growth of "virtual mobility," the use of the internet to deliver courses anywhere in the world to anyone who has access to a computer and modem. Among the many challenges of internet-based education are monitoring of quality and equity of access. One creative response to both challenges has been the "open courseware" offered by the Massachusetts Institute of Technology (MIT), which posted hundreds of its courses online and made them available without cost to anyone in the world. Other universities around the globe are also developing creative ways of delivering education remotely and reaching students and professionals who may never have considered studying abroad. The internet can also be an invaluable tool for alumni of study abroad programs to stay in touch with their host campuses once they return home and to benefit from the continuing educational opportunities available online. The Erasmus student of the 21st century will look quite different from her ancestor, with an iPod loaded with courses from dozens of universities, as well as a well-worn passport that includes short- and long-term international academic sojourns abroad and frequent mobility throughout her professional career.

NOTES

[1] Education at a Glance, OECD.

[2] Global Education Digest 2008, Unesco Institute for Statistics (UIS).

[3] See http://opendoors.iienetwork.org.

[4] See http://atlas.iienetwork.org.

[5] Projected numbers for these countries are based on reports in national and international media.

[6] See the Observatory on Borderless Higher Education (OBHE): www.obhe.ac.uk.

[7] We do not provide a detailed summary of the brain-drain debate here as this topic has been covered extensively in other publications. See, for example, Docquier & Marfouk, 2004 and Kapur & McHale, 2005.

[8] See www.kaust.edu.sa.

REFERENCES

Adams, J.D., Black, G.C., Clemmons, J.R., & Stephan, P.E. (2004). *Scientific teams and institutional collaborations: Evidence from U.S. universities, 1981-1999.* (NBER Working paper no. 10640).

Altbach, P.G. (2007). *Tradition and transition: The international imperative in higher education.* Boston, MA: Center for International Higher Education, Boston College.

Altbach, P.G., & Knight, J. (2007). Higher education's landscape of internationalization: motivations and realities. In Altbach, P.G., *Tradition and transition: The international imperative in higher education.* Boston, MA: Center for International Higher Education, Boston College.

Anderson, S. (2004). *The multiplier effect.* Arlington, VA: National Foundation of American Policy. Retrieved from www.nfap.com/researchactivities/studies/TheMultiplierEffectNFAP.pdf

Atlas of Global Student Mobility. (2007). Retrieved from http://atlas.iienetwork.org

Atta-ur-Rahman. (2007). Higher education in Pakistan: A silent revolution. *IIENetworker*, Spring 2007, 36-39.

Banks, M., & Olsen, A. (2008). *Defining and measuring global student mobility: An Australian perspective.* Paper presented at the NAFSA Annual Conference 2008 Special Research Seminar, Washington, DC. IDP Education Pty Ltd.

Bhandari, R., & Chow, P. (2008). *Open Doors 2008: Report on International Educational Exchange.* New York: Institute of International Education.

Blumenthal, P. (2002). Virtual and physical mobility: a view from the U.S. In Wächter, B. (Ed.), *The virtual challenge to international cooperation in higher education. ACA papers on international cooperation.* Bonn, Germany: Lemmens.

Bohm, A., Davis, D., Meares, D., & Pearce, D. (2002). *Global student mobility 2025: Forecast of the demand for international higher education.* Sydney, Australia: IDP Education Australia.

Docquier, F., & Marfouk, A. (2004). *Measuring the international mobility of skilled workers (1990-2000): Release 1.0.* (World Bank Policy Research Working Paper No. 3381).

Finn, M.G. (2007). *Stay rates of foreign doctorate recipients from U.S. universities, 2005.* Oak Ridge, TN: Oak Ridge Institute for Science and Education.

Gray, D. (2006). *Global engagement in a virtual world.* Paper presented at the Assuring a Globally Engaged Science and Engineering Workforce Workshop, National Science Foundation, Washington DC, September 20-22.

Jonkers, K. (2004). *The role of return migrants in the development of Beijing's plan biotechnological cluster.* Paper presented for the Second Globelics Conference: Innovation Systems and Development, Beijing, October 16-20.

Kapur, D., & McHale, J. (2005). *Give us your best and brightest: the global hunt for talent and its impact on the developing world.* Washington, DC: Center for Global Development.

Knight, J. (2006a). *Internationalization of higher education: new directions, new challenges. 2005 IAU Global Survey Report.* Paris, France: International Association of Universities.

Knight, J. (2006b). Crossborder education: an analytical framework for program and provider mobility. In J.C. Smart (Ed.), *Higher education: Handbook of theory and research, 21* (pp. 345-395). Dordrecht, The Netherlands: Springer.

Lowell, L.B. (2001). *Policy responses to the international mobility of skilled labour.* International Migration Papers, 45 (December). Geneva: International Migration Branch. Retrieved from www.ilo.org/public/english/protection/migrant/download/imp/imp45.pdf

Meyer, J.B., & Brown, M. (1999). *Scientific diasporas: A new approach to the brain drain.* Paper presented for the World Conference on Science, UNESCO-ICSU, Budapest, 26 June-1 July.

National Science Board. (2008). *Science and Engineering Indicators 2008* (Vols. 1-2). Arlington, VA: National Science Foundation.

National Science Foundation. (2000). *Graduate education reform in Europe, Asia, and the Americas and international mobility of scientists and engineers.* Proceedings of an NSF Workshop, Division of Science Resources Studies, Directorate for Social, Behavioral, and Economic Sciences, National Science Foundation.

Reindl, R. (2007). *Hitting home: Quality, cost, and access challenges confronting higher education today.* Making Opportunity Affordable Initiative, the Lumina Foundation. Retrieved from www.makingopportunityaffordable.org/wp-content/file_uploads/Hitting_Home_030107.pdf

Teferra, D. (2005). Brain circulation: Unparalleled opportunities, underlying challenges, and outmoded presumptions. *Journal of Studies in International Education,* 9(3), 229-250.

Thorn, K., & Holm-Nielsen, L. B. (2006). *International mobility of researchers and scientists: Policy options for turning a drain into a gain.* (United Nations University-World Institute for Development Economics Research. Research Paper No. 2006/83). Retrieved from www.wider.unu.edu/publications/rps/rps2006/rp2006-83.pdf

UNESCO. (2008). *Global Education Digest 2008: Comparing education statistics across the world.* Montreal, Canada: UNESCO Institute for Statistics.

UNESCO. (2006). *Global Education Digest 2006: Comparing education statistics across the world.* Montreal, Canada: UNESCO Institute for Statistics.

Verbik, L., & Merkley, C. (2006). *The international branch campus: Models and trends.* London: The Observatory on Borderless Higher Education.

Wadhwa, V., Saxenian, A., Rissing, B., & Gereffi, G. (2007). *America's New Immigrant Entrepreneurs, Part I.* Duke Science, Technology & Innovation Paper No. 23. Available at http://ssrn.com/abstract=990152

Zweig, D., Changgui, C., & Rosen, S. (2004). Globalization and transnational human capital: Overseas and returnee scholars to China. *The China Quarterly, 179*, 735-757.

Chapter Two

GATS AND TRANSNATIONAL MOBILITY IN HIGHER EDUCATION

BY N.V. VARGHESE, INTERNATIONAL INSTITUTE FOR EDUCATIONAL PLANNING, UNESCO

Higher education, in the context of globalization, has become a market-driven activity to promote an international and multicultural outlook among graduates to suit the requirements of a global labor market centered on knowledge production. Institutions of higher education have not only become global in their orientation and operation but have also become yet another sector offering investment opportunities for producing and selling a good or service for the global market. Market orientation and profitability are replacing the national concerns and social functions of institutions of higher education.

The General Agreement on Trade in Services (GATS) represents a set of multilateral rules for trade in services. It covers all internationally traded services including education. Within education, higher education is more amenable to trade than other lower levels of education. Many countries are part of GATS, and cross-border mobility in higher education is facilitated under the GATS framework, although transnational mobility extends beyond those countries that are signatories of GATS. Transnational education implies the mobility of students, teachers, institutions and programs crossing national boundaries. The providers at times behave more as investors than as educators, attracted to the sector to do business and earn a profit. Given the potential profitability of the sector, there is competition among institutions to be part of transnational higher education.

This chapter analyzes transnational higher education with specific reference to the transnational mobility of students, teachers and institutions. The first section briefly discusses the shift in emphasis from aid to trade in promoting development, followed by an introduction to some features of GATS in section two. Section three discusses institutional mobility, while sections four and five deal with issues related to teacher and student mobility. Section six draws some conclusions.

From Aid to Trade in Development

It was argued in the 1950s and 1960s that because poor countries are trapped in low level equilibrium, they cannot develop without external assistance. Capital was considered to be the missing link, and external aid has been the central policy instrument of the international community to promote economic development in poor countries (Van de Walle, 2005). This model of development assistance came under attack in the 1990s for various reasons.

First, the capital flows were from developed to developing countries. However, the underlying expectation that returns to investment and growth rates would be higher in developing countries in order to catch-up with the developed countries and would ultimately lead to a convergence of income levels did not materialize. Therefore, the effectiveness of aid as an instrument of development assistance was questioned. Second, this period also coincided with the decline of the state and ascendancy of the market in development.

The market operates on the basis of prices and profits. Taxpayers in rich countries were less willing to use their income to subsidize development in developing countries. The prevailing market ideology in the development field did not encourage aid, which was perceived as a non-market-based development strategy. Third, the political argument for aid was to check the spread of a competing ideology. With the collapse of the USSR, the argument for containing communism lost its value. On all counts, aid declined and was less than the committed share for most of the developed countries (Degenbol-Martinussen & Engberg-Pedersen, 2003). Foreign direct investment increased during this period. This changing political orientation contributed to the expansion of market forces and the extension of trade to sectors such as education.

Liberalization policies adopted by many developing countries resulted in the opening of their markets to foreign investments and facilitated the easy inflow of foreign capital. In the process, trade became the more important and prominent player in development, with the World Trade Organization (WTO) setting the parameters that would govern trade in goods. As a consequence of the rapid growth of the service sector in most developed countries, it is estimated that services now account for the largest share of the global output and employment and for a good share of merchandise exports (Chanda, 2002). Although the service sector emerged as an important sector in production and exports, services were never part of any trade negotiations until the establishment of GATS in 1995.

Education became one of the services included in trade negotiations under GATS. It can be argued that trade in education has an adverse effect on development assistance to education. Countries engaged in trade in education have reduced the share of development assistance allocated to post-secondary education, while countries such as Sweden and Denmark, which do not trade in education, have increased their support of post-secondary education. It seems that developed countries are viewing trade as more effective and more development-friendly than development assistance (Vincent-Lancrin, 2005).

Some Features of Trade in Services Under GATS

GATS represents a set of multilateral rules governing international trade in services. GATS covers all internationally traded services and, in total, covers 12 different service sectors including education. Within the education sector, GATS covers five categories of education services: primary, secondary, higher, adult and others. Trade in education under the GATS framework takes place in four modes: 1) cross-border supply of the service—where consumers remain within the country; 2) consumption abroad—where the consumers (students) cross the border; 3) commercial presence of the provider in another country—institutional mobility; 4) presence of persons in another country—staff mobility (Knight, 2002).

The GATS rules include both unconditional and conditional obligations. The unconditional obligations include the most favored nation (MFN) treatment. It implies the nondiscrimination principle or equal treatment of all trading partners from all WTO members. Each country has the option to keep a service in or out of international trade. However, if a service is included in the trading, then equal opportunities should be given to all trading partners.

The conditional obligations include market access and national treatment. Market access implies the degree to which domestic market access is granted to foreign providers of any service covered under GATS. In this case, a country has the option to limit or expand its commitment to grant market access in a selected service sector. A country can decide which service sector it wants to provide market access to. Even within a selected sector, the host country can incorporate restrictions on: 1) the number of foreign service suppliers; 2) the value of transactions or assets; 3) the total quantity of the output; 4) the number of nationals to be employed; and 5) the extent of foreign capital participation.

Progressive trade liberalization is another governing principle in GATS. Trade liberalization can be made specific for each service sector and also for each mode of supply. Experience has shown that some sectors are more favored for trade liberalization than others. Tourism-related sectors are more trade liberalization-friendly than other sectors such as health, education, postal services, etc. (Chanda, 2002). Although fewer countries have agreed to include education under GATS, in some education accounts for a large share of total exports. There is competition among providers to offer courses in developing countries and among institutions to attract teachers and students from developing countries. The rest of the chapter focuses on the three key forms of cross-border transactions—at the level of institutions, faculty and students—that are most likely to be affected by GATS.

Transnational Institutional Mobility

Institutional mobility takes place in different forms such as branch campuses and franchising or twinning arrangements. Branch campuses are an important and recent visible form of institutional mobility. Franchising denotes the delivery of all or part of a course in an institution other than that in which it is developed and validated. Twinning denotes a situation where the program and its delivery are jointly conducted between institutions in the home country and host country. Although franchising and twinning are less visible than branch campuses, they are quantitatively larger segments of institutional mobility (Martin, 2007).

Examples of institutional mobility are many. Universities from Australia, the UK, the U.S., and other countries open branch campuses in many developing countries. Some of the developing countries have branch campuses of several foreign universities and institutes. For example, Malaysia has branch campuses of universities including the University of Nottingham (United Kingdom), Monash University and Curtin University of Technology (Australia), etc. (Sirat, 2006). Similarly, Singapore has branch campuses of the Johns Hopkins University and the University of Chicago (United States), INSEAD (France), and Shanghai Jiao Tong University (China). Monash University, Bond University (Australia) and Business School Netherlands have branch campuses in several countries of Africa.

Countries such as China permit only collaborative arrangements, in which foreign institutions must act in collaboration with national/domestic institutions. Countries such as South Africa insist that for-profit universities register under the Companies Act. In 1999, there were five education companies in South Africa listed in the Johannesburg Stock Exchange (JSE). These five companies owned 43 institutions, and 145 institutions applied for registration to the Department of Education. However, some companies were de-listed and, by 2004, only two companies—Advtech and Nasper—were listed in the JSE, and they accounted for more than 70 percent of enrollment in private higher education institutions in South Africa (Mabizela, 2006).

Many transnational providers operate through private institutions. Collaboration with foreign universities and institutions helps the local private universities. In some cases, it helps them to obtain academic credibility, quality appeal, and also permits them to levy high fees. It helps some universities to levy fees in foreign currencies.

Many transnational institutions offer courses in limited subject areas. They offer market-friendly courses to cater to the private business enterprises—foreign or national. Courses in business administration, computer science, accounting, marketing, economics, communication, etc., are very common in such institutions (Varghese, 2009). Further, since fees are the main source of income for transnational institutions, especially those that are not affiliated to religious agencies, they levy high fees that result in greater inequities and lack of access to higher education for the poor.

Southeast Asian governments in Malaysia and Singapore have invited foreign universities to start branch campuses in order to make the country a hub for international education. At times, a foreign provider also helps to bypass the national regulations regarding medium of instruction and national curriculum.

Transnational Teacher Mobility

International migration is often viewed as an economically rewarding activity, especially in the context of globalization. Studies show large income gains from global labor migration (Rosenzweig, 2004). According to some estimates, a migration of one million college graduates to the U.S. will increase the global income by $1.4 billion each year. Some other studies have shown that unrestricted migration could more than double the global GDP (Martin, 2004). Teacher mobility, especially between countries, has increased in the recent past. Faculty go abroad in part due to teacher shortages in the destination country and also because host institutions perceive that hosting a teacher from another country can enhance their international character, especially in the context of globalization and competing for students and resources.

Some developed countries, including the UK and the U.S., face a shortage of teachers primarily due to the lack of attractiveness of the profession. With the emergence of new employment opportunities provided by private and transnational corporations, the attractiveness of teaching in the not-for-profit education sector has further been eroded. A study on teacher shortages in the UK has shown that "salaries and working conditions of teachers have never been fully adjusted to take into account the fact that teaching these days has to compete in an open market for graduates" (Smithers and Robinson, 1998, p. 2). In developing African countries, on the other hand, different factors come into play: large-scale natural disasters, political instability, and the widespread AIDS epidemic have led to a shortage of teachers (De Villiers, 2007).

Wage differentials, professional enrichment, and opportunities to travel abroad are important motivations for teachers to move from one country to another (Morgan, et al., 2006). A French survey in 2001 categorized four types of professors based on their motivations to migrate to other countries: 1) professors who have a purely local career who do not like to migrate; 2) professors with an international career but with a local bias who would like to settle down in their own country; 3) professors who have never taught abroad but would like to migrate and return to the home country; and 4) professors who have a purely international career—those who have worked abroad and would like to stay abroad forever. A large share of migration belongs to the third group, those who would like to work abroad for a limited number of years and return to their home countries.

There were large-scale recruitments of teachers from Caribbean countries, such as Jamaica, to the UK and the U.S., and from African countries, such as South Africa, to the UK. Such migrations led to teacher shortages in the sending countries. The teacher shortages in the sending countries became so acute that some of them accused the developed countries of "raiding [their] resources" and demanded compensation from the UK and U.S. governments (Appleton, et al., 2006). The bilateral discussions to resolve the issue resulted in an agreement to develop a strategy of "managed migration" that put an end to the large-scale recruitment of teachers (Morgan, et al., 2006). The mass recruitment and resultant shortages of teachers in the sending countries became an important agenda item at the Commonwealth Education Ministers' Conference held in Edinburgh in 2003, which led to developing a Commonwealth protocol on teacher recruitment.

Teacher migration is not always from developing to developed countries. Teachers move within developed countries and among developing countries. Teachers from Australia, Canada, and New Zealand are found in the UK. Teachers from India, Kenya, Zambia, and Zimbabwe are found in Botswana, for example. However, large-scale migration still continues to be from developing to developed countries.

Teacher mobility takes different forms. Many universities have departments specializing in regional studies—departments of African, Asian or Latin American studies. These departments attract teachers from their regions of specialty. For example, the Center for Latin American Studies of the University of Chicago attracts at least three visiting professors every year under the Tinker Visiting Professor program. More than 30 professors from Latin America have visited and taught at the university this decade. Many similar examples can be found at other universities in the developed world.

In some cases, teacher migration is in selected subject areas. It is estimated that more than 10,000 Indian teachers work in U.S. universities. Indian professors, including some Nobel laureates, are engaged in research and teaching activities predominantly in science, engineering and social science subject areas (Melwani, 2007). Many of these teachers have obtained their doctoral degrees from U.S. universities and have stayed on in the U.S. to teach.

Under the Erasmus Mundus program, more than 1,000 university teachers from developing counties came to Europe between 2004 and 2008. Under the same program, efforts have been made to establish collaborative arrangements to promote student and staff mobility between 12 European and eight Indian universities (EurAsia News, 2008). Professor Rick Trainor, President of the higher education action group Universities UK, led a delegation of UK Vice-Chancellors to India to discuss institutional collaborations and student and teacher mobility between premier institutions in India and the UK (International, 2008).

Some universities appoint foreign professors to improve their image and international competitiveness to promote research, improve the quality of teaching, and attract foreign students. For example, the Ministry of Human Resource Development of Korea plans to recruit 300 foreign professors in the coming years. The proposal indicates that "It is part of our efforts to enhance the quality of education at national universities to meet the global standard" (Kim, 2007). This does not include decisions by individual universities to recruit foreign professors. For example, Seoul National University (SNU), a state-funded university, is planning to recruit 150 professors to promote its international competitiveness. Further, candidates who possess the necessary language proficiency to lecture in English are at an advantage when SNU is hiring native Korean professors (Korean Times, 2001).

Transnational Student Mobility

One of the important components of cross-border education involves the movement of students from domestic to foreign countries. Only a small number of students in the past crossed borders to pursue higher education. This number has increased recently; nearly 2.9 million students pursued cross-border education in 2006 (OECD, 2008), and this number is projected to rise to 7.2 million by 2025 (Bohm, et al., 2002).

The market for cross-border students accounts for billions of dollars, hence there is competition among higher education institutions to attract foreign students and to generate income and profit. The most familiar direction of cross-border student flow is from developing to developed countries. According to UNESCO Institute for Statistics (UIS) data (2007), North America and Western Europe continue to be favorite destinations for most students from any region, apart from students from Central Asia who tend to go to the Russian Federation or other Eastern European countries. Nearly three-fourths of internationally mobile students from all regions, except Central and East Asia and the Pacific, seek higher education in OECD countries. Nearly 90 percent of students from North America and Europe cross the border to study in another country of the same region; 80 percent of students from Latin America travel to North America and Western Europe for their studies. A large number of students from China travel to Japan, and those from India and Indonesia often travel to Australia. However, even in all these cases, except in Central Asia, the flow is from developing to developed countries—OECD countries.

The U.S. attracts the single-largest share of foreign students (20 percent) followed by the UK (13 percent), Germany (8 percent), France (8 percent), Australia (7 percent), China (7 percent), Canada (5 percent) and Japan (4 percent) (IIE, 2007). Australia experienced a rapid expansion in foreign student numbers in the 1990s, and New Zealand has had the same experience this decade. Although the in-flow of foreign students is highest to the U.S., it accounts for less than 3.4 percent of total tertiary enrollments in the U.S. The share of foreign students, according to the OECD (2008), to the total enrollment is 28.5 percent in New Zealand, 20.9 percent in Australia, 17.9 percent in the UK, 14.2 percent in Canada, 11.4 percent in Germany, and about 11.2 percent in France. This shows that foreign students in smaller countries account for a large share of their tertiary enrollment. The cross-border student flow is higher at the research level. In countries such as New Zealand and the UK, more than two-thirds of the students engaged in research-level studies are from foreign countries.

A large majority of students, especially in Anglophone countries, choose business, technical and scientific fields of study while in non-Anglophone countries, such as France, a larger share of international students pursue higher education in arts and humanities.

Ten host countries, together, account for nearly 72 percent of all cross-border student activity, regardless of the direction of the flow. Most of the developed countries are host countries, while most of the developing countries are sending countries. Countries such as China, India and Korea send a large number of students abroad. Countries such as Australia, France, Germany, the UK and the U.S. are the major host countries. Asian countries top the list of sending countries with a share of 45.3 percent of students, followed by Europe (23 percent), Africa (9.9 percent), South America (5 percent), North America (3.5 percent), etc. (OECD, 2008).

There have been some changes in the destination of cross-border students in the recent past. There are winners and losers in terms of the cross-border market share. There have been declines in the market share of the two most significant players—the UK and the U.S.—followed by Canada. The biggest gains in the late 1990s were in Australia, and now the biggest gains seem to be in New Zealand. France, Italy and South Africa have also improved their market shares.

More than 73 percent of all Asian students study in three English-speaking countries—Australia, the UK and the U.S. The share of Chinese students going to the U.S. has been more than halved—from 60 percent in 1995 to 26 percent in 2004. Japan and India, too, have seen reductions in the share of their students going to the U.S. In the case of India, the decline is around 14 percentage points. The decline in the share of Japanese students in the U.S. is not substantial—3.2 percentage points (Varghese, 2008). The biggest gainer of cross-border education seems to be Australia in the 1990s and New Zealand this decade.

Concluding Observations

Education is a significant variable in determining national income and personal earnings. Since inequalities in education can lead to future economic and social inequalities, it is important from the societal point of view to ensure that educational opportunities are distributed equally. The demand for and supply of a good or a service in a market depends on prices and profits that, very often, are not the most reliable instruments to ensure equity. Cross-border trade in education depends on the profitability of investment in this segment; hence, trade may not necessarily be the most desirable mechanism to promote equity in educational development.

Higher education systems in developing countries, especially in Africa, are still too small and need state support for their expansion. Given the low level of household income, a large expansion of higher education through private or transnational institutions is a difficult proposition. Public intervention is needed in these countries to expand higher education to support students coming from households with less paying capacity to pursue higher education.

Transnational education may lead to brain drain. Since individuals seek transnational education at a high cost, they may try to maximize their returns from the investment. They are potential migrants to the host countries or to multinational corporations where salary levels are high. Although they may be sending remittances, their contribution to national development is reduced, if not lost.

It is often argued that when transnational providers enter the national scene through trade, it forces competition among unequals—between institutions from developed and developing countries—which may weaken national institutions. The transnational segment of the educational market may attract people with paying capacity, leaving the public institutions as the reserve for the poor, may distort national priorities, and may result in the further weakening of public institutions of higher education.

Given these factors, it is not an easy decision to welcome transnational education in many countries. In principle, countries that are signatory to the GATS have the freedom to decide upon the service that is to be opened up for trade depending upon whether or not the terms of trade are in their favor. The fact that the number of countries committed to trade in education is less than the number of signatories to GATS reflects the complexities of opening the education sector to markets and trade. What is becoming more acceptable nowadays is regulated growth and expansion of transnational education.

Regulation is a way of protecting national interests and students' interest even when the sector is opened for trade as part of GATS. The experience varies among countries with regard to the type of regulations for trading in services. There are countries that have too few regulations, while others have too many (Varghese, 2007). Countries such as France, Germany, Nigeria, and Russia have the fewest regulations, and countries such as Cyprus, South Africa, and UAE have the strictest and most numerous restrictions, including in the area of accreditation of programs and curricula (Verbik, et al, 2005). Experience shows that too few regulations, or a lack of them, will distort the national concerns, and too much regulation will drive the cross-border providers away to other destinations.

There is growing demand for regulatory frameworks to govern trade in education at the regional and international levels, in order to supplement existing frameworks at the national level. The Code of Good Practice in the Provision of Transnational Education was established by the Council of Europe in cooperation with UNESCO; it protects students from fraudulent degrees and qualifications (Verbik, et al, 2005). UNESCO and OECD have developed a set of guidelines for quality provision in cross-border higher education (UNESCO/OECD, 2005). Yet another set produced jointly by UNESCO and the Commonwealth of Learning provides more detailed guidelines for countries entering GATS negotiations (Knight, 2006).

Based on the experience of different countries and the prevalence of fraudulent practices, there is need for regulation in certain areas such as: 1) granting permission for the establishment and operation of cross-border institutions; 2) types of courses offered to prevent the lopsided development of education; 3) regulating the award and recognition of degrees; and 4) the maximum amount of fees that can be levied. These regulations are needed to develop an equitable system of higher education.

Finally, it is often pointed out that trade and market operations in education benefit some groups more than others. Therefore, it is important to identify the winners and losers in an educational process mediated through the market. Further, public interventions and regulatory mechanisms are needed to make trade in education more gentle and educational markets more people-friendly. Regulations help provide students with protection, reinforce confidence in market operations, and make markets more acceptable by extending their social role.

REFERENCES

Appleton, S., Morgan, J. & Sives, A. (2006). Should teachers stay at home? The impact of international teacher mobility. *Journal of Internal Development, 18,* 771-786.

Bohm, A., Davies, A., Meares, D., & Pearce, D. (2002). *Global student mobility.* Sydney: IDP Education.

Chanda, R. (2002). *GATS and its implications for developing countries: Key issues and concerns.* DESA Discussion Paper No.2. New York: Department of Economic and Social Affairs, UN.

Degenbol-Martinussen, J., & Engberg-Pedersen, P. (2003). *Aid: Understanding international development cooperation.* London: Z Books Limited.

De Villiers, R. (2007). Migration from developing countries: The case of South African teachers to the United Kingdom. *Perspectives in Education, 25:2,* 67-76.

Institute of International Education. (2007). *Atlas of student mobility.* New York: IIE.

Kim, T. (2007, August 22). Universities to recruit 300 foreign professors, *The Korea Times.* Retrieved February 19, 2009, from www.koreatimes.co.kr/www/news/nation/2007/08/113_8801.html

Knight, J. (2002). *Trade in higher education services: Implications of GATS.* London: Observatory on Borderless Education.

Knight, J. (2006). *Higher education crossing borders: A guide to the implications of the GATS for cross-border education.* Paris: UNESCO/Commonwealth of Learning.

Mabizela, M. (2006). Recounting the state of private higher education in South Africa. In Varghese, N.V. (Ed.), *Growth and expansion of higher education in Africa* (pp.131-166). Paris: IIEP/UNESCO.

Martin, M. (Ed.). (2007). *Cross-border higher education: Regulation, quality assurance and impact* (Vol.1). Paris: IIEP.

Martin, P.L. (2004). Migration. In Lomborg, B. (Ed.), *Global crises, global solutions* (pp. 443-477). Cambridge, UK: Cambridge University Press.

Melwani, L. (2007, January 2). Academic stars. *Little India.* Retrieved February 19, 2009, from www.littleindia.com/news/142/ARTICLE/1465/2007-01-02.html

Morgan, W.J., Sives, A., & Appleton, S. (2006). *Teacher mobility, 'brain drain,' labor markets and educational resources in the Commonwealth,* Research Issue no.66. London: Department for International Development (DFID).

Organisation for Economic Co-operation and Development. (2008). *Education at a glance 2008*. Paris: OECD.

Rosenzweig, M. (2004). Migration. In Lomborg, B. (Ed.), *Global crises, global solutions* (pp. 478-488). Cambridge, UK: Cambridge University Press.

Scafidi, B., Sjoquist, D.L., & Stinebrickner, T.R. (2007). Race, poverty and teacher mobility. *Economics of Education Review, 26*, 145-159.

Sirat, M. (2006). Malaysia. In UNESCO and RIHED (Eds.), *Higher education in South-East Asia* (pp.101-136). Bangkok: UNESCO.

Smithers, A., & Robinson, P. (1998). *Teacher supply 1998, passing problem or impending crisis*. Liverpool: Centre for Education and Employment, University of Liverpool.

UIS: UNESCO Institute of Statistics. (2007). *Global Education Digest*. Montreal: UIS.

UNESCO/OECD: United Nations Educational, Scientific and Cultural Organization/ Organisation for Economic Co-operation and Development. (2005). *Guidelines for quality provision in cross-border higher education*. Paris: UNESCO/OECD.

Van de Walle, N. (2005). *Overcoming stagnation in aid dependent countries*. Washington, DC: Centre for Global Development.

Varghese, N.V. (2007). GATS and national regulatory policies in higher education: Guidelines for developing countries. Research paper series. Paris: IIEP/UNESCO.

Varghese, N.V. (2008). Globalization of higher education and cross-border student mobility. Research paper series. Paris: IIEP/UNESCO.

Varghese, N.V. (2009). Cross-border higher education and national systems of education. In Field, M.H., & Fegan, J. (Eds.), *Education across borders: Politics, policy and legislative action*. Berlin: Springer.

Verbik, L., & Jokivirta, L. (2005). *National regulatory framework for transactional higher education: Models and trends*. London: The Observatory on Borderless Higher Education.

Vincent-Lancrin, S. (2005). Building capacity through cross-border higher education. In Vincent-Lancrin, S., Hopper, R., & Grosso, M.G. *Cross-border higher education for development*. Paris: OECD/World Bank.

Chapter Three

INTERNATIONALIZING THE ACADEMY: THE IMPACT OF SCHOLAR MOBILITY

BY SABINE O'HARA, COUNCIL FOR INTERNATIONAL EXCHANGE OF SCHOLARS, A DIVISION OF THE INSTITUTE OF INTERNATIONAL EDUCATION

Introduction

Faculty and PhD students have long crossed national borders in pursuit of a better education and opportunities for advancing their scholarly work and research networks. Scholars tend to be a part of the group of people that Harm De Blij (2008) calls "globals," as opposed to "mobals" and "locals." Globals easily move across national borders and cultural context and are a part of global networks of professional contacts and activities.[1] Locals are those who do not have the opportunity to escape their immediate contexts and pressures. Mobals—a portmanteau of the terms mobile and global/local—occupy somewhat of an in-between position, as their name suggests. They may or may not cross national borders, yet their migration is often driven by economic need and survival and does not come with the same level of access and opportunity as that of the globals.

Faculty members and PhD students most closely fit the description of the globals. Yet even for scholars the world is not completely flat, and borders often continue to demarcate extensive, tangible differences in work environments, infrastructure, resources and opportunity. In some countries and regions, scholars face shortages in electricity and supplies and are persecuted for speaking their mind and exposing others to current scientific knowledge, while in other countries and regions, scholars enjoy a high degree of independence and academic freedom and have access to state-of-the-art equipment and up-to-date information. These differences contribute to scholar mobility and at the same time result in uneven patterns of scholar mobility. Some scholars become mobile in order to gain new knowledge and advance research and teaching methods; others desire economic advancement or seek to escape reprisal and violence.

And scholar mobility continues to evolve. Knowledge has become more portable in the internet age; large databases are now accessible in real time around the globe, knowledge is exchanged no longer bilaterally but in multifaceted knowledge networks, and scholarly collaboration takes place not only within the more traditional venue of the university but also increasingly in private sector research institutes and industry labs. These developments make it challenging to track the mobility of scholars and scholarly collaboration. Collaboration no longer depends on the physical proximity of the collaborators but can take place among multiple collaborators, locations and academic disciplines.

This chapter examines the characteristics of scholar mobility and its main impacts. Its starting point is a categorization of the complex impacts of scholar mobility, followed by a description of scholar mobility to and from the U.S., which continues to be the largest receiving country for scholars and students. The analysis draws in part on data and case study examples from the Fulbright Scholar Program, the flagship international exchange program of the U.S. government.[2] The chapter concludes with a brief review of impending changes to scholar mobility given the significant impact of technology and the growing portability of scholarly work.

Defining Scholar Mobility and its Impact

Scholar mobility is difficult to measure. The common definition of scholar mobility as the movement of scholars across national borders tends to capture primarily those scholars who are affiliated with a host university or research institute in their destination country. Scholars who pursue professional activities outside the official channels of institutional affiliations, who conduct field work, data collection or other research on their own, who collaborate with colleagues through informal arrangements, or who guest lecture at a colleague's invitation are not counted. Scholars who move from one institution to another within their home country, such as the growing ranks of adjunct faculty, also remain uncounted in scholar mobility figures. The estimated under-counting of scholar mobility is therefore especially significant at the postdoctoral level, when scholars no longer pursue a formal degree or credit-bearing coursework that would require them to matriculate at a degree-granting host institution.

The work of scholars is both essential and uncomfortable. Scholarship is about discovery, integration, creative engagement and thoughtful application of knowledge—that is, of what we understand to be true about our world, about human experience and culture, and about that which transcends both. While this pursuit of knowledge may have different motivations—some may seek better economic conditions, and others prestige, the advancement of skills, or the engagement of future generations in the pursuit of knowledge—the work of scholars acknowledges that our human understanding is always partial, always prone to error, and always in need of re-visioning and innovation. The work of scholars is therefore a key driver of progress, innovation and improved human and economic capacity. Yet the work of scholars also questions the status quo and raises at times uncomfortable subjects.

In response to this tension, scholars have long argued for the protection of academic freedom and free inquiry and have objected to narrow definitions of "acceptable" scholarly pursuits. These protections remain elusive in some parts of the world, and a segment of scholar mobility remains involuntary as scholars are persecuted for their pursuit, defense and dissemination of knowledge.[3] Data provided by the Scholar Rescue Fund, an IIE initiative that provides fellowships for established scholars whose lives and work are threatened in their home countries, shows that the largest group of scholars facing reprisal comes from sub-Saharan Africa, with the Middle East/North Africa region coming in a close second. These two regions of the world account for 61 percent of scholars who applied to the Scholar Rescue Fund between 2002 and 2007 and for almost three-quarters of all grantees (73 percent). Since its founding in 2002, the Scholar Rescue Fund has placed 266 scholars from almost every academic discipline at over 135 institutions in 31 countries. Table 3.1 lists the relative representation of world regions among rescued scholars.[4]

TABLE 3.1: SCHOLAR MOBILITY RECORDED BY WORLD REGION (2002-07)

World Region	% of All Applicants	% of All Grantees
Sub-Saharan Africa	38%	42%
Middle East/North Africa	23%	31%
Asia and the Pacific	24%	13%
Europe and Eurasia	11%	11%
Central and Latin America	4%	3%

Source: IIE Scholar Rescue Fund. Jarecki, H. & Kaisth, D. (2009). *Scholar rescue in the modern world.* New York, NY: Institute of International Education.

Scholars have a broad impact on the academy and society at large, yet their impact is often difficult to calculate because of the immense variety in their work. The complex roles of the scholar have their reflection in equally complex patterns of mobility. In addition to world region of origin, research shows that academic field is a significant factor influencing scholar mobility and the degree to which scholars engage in research, teaching and other aspects of their work.[5] In the case of U.S. faculty, the type of academic institution with which a scholar is affiliated is another important variable.[6] Yet regardless of these distinctions, scholars impact society in three main ways:

- Scholars advance knowledge across the spectrum of academic disciplines including the applied fields;

- Scholars influence students and shape future generations of leaders and scholars;

- Scholars translate and disseminate knowledge and serve as a resource to the public and private sector, to the media, and to civic organizations.

Mobility is a key component enabling scholars to fulfill these roles and advance their impact in each of these areas, as the following three sections illustrate.

Knowledge Transfer and Innovation

Scholar mobility has long been a key factor in advancing knowledge and bringing about progress. Universities functioned as global institutions from the very beginning. In the West, Latin was their common language, facilitating communication among professors and students from many different countries and cultures. The knowledge they imparted reflected scholarly learning in the Western world rather than the knowledge of a single country or world region. Non-Western traditions were also shaped by scholar mobility, although colonization spread the Western university model around the globe. U.S. universities, too, were influenced by multiple strands of mobility, from the original colonial model imported from England to the strong impact of the idea of the German research university in the 19th century.[7]

Even today, there is a recognition that scholar mobility advances the objectives of the academy. Scholars from different educational systems and cultural backgrounds advance research questions, methodological approaches and epistemological frameworks; and while visiting scholars to the U.S. undoubtedly benefit from the infrastructure and resources available at U.S. institutions, U.S. institutions and scholars also benefit significantly from the perspectives, research methods and skills visiting scholars bring to the U.S. A recent Universities UK report acknowledges this impact of scholar mobility:

> Enhanced researcher mobility allows for new ways of thinking to develop, and supports the academy in its pursuit of greater knowledge and new discoveries. Institutions benefit from students and staff who approach issues differently, and who are committed to greater collaboration with colleagues in other countries and thereby add value to research teams. Individuals benefit from new experiences, learning different ways of designing research projects, and gaining access to new kinds of research equipment and different opportunities. Networks created through researcher mobility can sustain the development of new disciplines and aid research and institutional links.[8]

Diverse perspectives, methodologies, and valuation frameworks are essential to the formation of a robust body of knowledge that advances overall knowledge formation. As knowledge systems become homogenized and "inbred," the likelihood of innovation, knowledge creation and creative knowledge application is reduced. For example, the loss of socio-diversity, "defined as the various social and economic arrangements by which people organize their societies, particularly the underlying assumptions, goals, values and social behaviors guiding these arrangements…,"[9] may pose as much of a risk to future solutions to social and environmental problems as the loss of bio-diversity. Scholar mobility contributes significantly to the knowledge transfer and methodological diversity that is at the heart of innovation and the advancement of knowledge.

U.S. scholars also report benefiting significantly from research and teaching experiences abroad and from access to information and observations in other countries that would not be accessible to them at home. Such access to first-hand, context based information is especially important to the advancement of knowledge that seeks solutions to such intractable problems as climate change, biodiversity loss, pandemics, negative social and environmental externalities of development, and decision-making under conditions of uncertainty.

Influencing Future Generations

Scholar mobility has long played an indispensable role in increasing the exposure of students to diverse methodological and didactic approaches and insights. Given their influence as teachers and mentors, scholars can support or hinder the increasingly important advancement of international awareness and cultural literacy among students. College and university students comprise the future economic, civic, cultural and political leadership of their countries. Given the increasingly global marketplace and world in which we live, these future leaders must do more than acquire knowledge in their chosen academic or professional field. They must also be globally aware, culturally literate and able to collaborate effectively across cultural, national and linguistic boundaries.[10]

This urgent need for increased global awareness and multicultural competency requires that faculty members who teach their countries' future leaders are themselves engaged in international collaboration. In its 2008 report *Mapping Internationalization on U.S. Campuses*, the American Council on Education states:

> Both ACE's experience working directly with institutions and the literature on internationalization show that faculty play the leading role in driving campus internationalization. It follows, therefore, that institutional investments in faculty travel to teach, conduct research, and lead students on education abroad programs, as well as workshops to help faculty internationalize their courses, can have a significant impact on internationalizing the curriculum.[11]

A study of returned U.S. Fulbright scholars, conducted by the Stanford Research Institute, confirms the critical role scholars play in shaping the international literacy of their campuses (see Table 3.2).

TABLE 3.2: KEY OUTCOMES ASSOCIATED WITH RETURNED U.S. FULBRIGHT SCHOLARS[12]

When Fulbright Scholars return to the U.S., they ...	
Share information about host country with colleagues	99%
Recommend that faculty colleagues apply for Fulbright	91%
Recommend other faculty international experiences	85%
Become more aware of cultural diversity	85%
Encourage students to study abroad	80%
Incorporate Fulbright experience into curricula or teaching methods	73%
Share information about host country with community groups	72%

Source: Stanford Research Institute, 2002

Shaping Public Perception

Given the high status scholars have in most societies, scholars influence public perception beyond their professional networks. The Fulbright Scholar Program, with its explicit goal of advancing mutual understanding between the people of the U.S. and the people of other nations, has long recognized the significant multiplier role of scholars. Despite the often significant time lag associated with the dispersal of knowledge from the academy to the public sphere, scholars influence knowledge formation. Scholars are often called upon by the media to comment on new discoveries or technological advancements; scholars are recruited as speakers by civic and community organizations, public libraries and schools; and scholars are tapped to lend their expertise in support of or against various policy positions—sometimes to their own detriment.

Returned U.S. Fulbright scholars often report surprise at the intense interest diverse audiences show in their work and in their accounts of life in the U.S. They also report the significant learning that took place during their experience overseas as they availed themselves of opportunities to address and interact with audiences on and off their host campus.

U.S. campuses and communities also report how valuable their interactions with visiting scholars are in expanding their insights and awareness of other cultures and countries. This learning and growth experience is particularly significant in small rural campuses and communities that tend to have less exposure to international diversity. Preconceptions and biases tend to be diminished, if not overcome, through personal contact with the medical professional from India, the teacher from the Philippines and the computer scientist from China.

The positive impact scholar mobility has on the advancement of knowledge, the international awareness of future generations, and public opinion about different cultures and countries is precisely why societies invest in scholar mobility. Scholar mobility is key to innovation, to advancing the social acceptance of knowledge, and to securing future economic success. A recent report to the European Parliament acknowledges the critical role of scholar mobility:

> Globalization is accelerating, and this has an impact on the way we produce, share and use knowledge. Major global challenges such as climate change, poverty, infectious disease, threats to energy, food and water supply, security of the citizen, networks security and the digital divide highlight the need for effective global S&T cooperation to promote sustainable development.... greater cross-border coordination of research investments and activities will increase Europe's competitiveness and its attractiveness as a place to invest in research and innovation.[13]

Measuring Scholar Mobility to and from the U.S.

With approximately 655,000 full-time faculty members and nearly 4,000 colleges and universities that vary significantly in size and degree level, the U.S. has the largest higher education capacity in the world. It is therefore not surprising that it is also a significant recipient of scholars from around the world. Yet outbound scholar numbers are relatively low, and U.S. scholars tend to be less mobile than their counterparts.[14] Only one-third of U.S. scholars reported that they had taken at least one trip abroad for study or research. This makes U.S. faculty the least mobile among faculty members in a study comparing mobility rates in fourteen countries.[15]

One indicator that researchers have used to assess the impact of scholar mobility across national borders is joint publications by scholars from different countries. The underlying assumption is that co-authorship has typically included some component of face-to-face collaboration and thus implies mobility across national borders. According to the National Science Board, 54 countries formed the core of scholarly collaboration measured in contributions to co-authored publications in 2000.[16] The contributions overwhelmingly involve partners from Europe: only six of the 54 are Central and Latin American countries, five are Asian, and only two are African.

What follows is a description of scholar mobility from the perspective of the U.S., starting with a discussion of scholar mobility into the U.S., and followed by a description of the outbound mobility of U.S. scholars.

Scholar Mobility to the U.S.

According to IIE's *Open Doors 2008: Report on International Educational Exchange*, in 2007/2008 an estimated 106,000 scholars taught and conducted research at over 400 colleges and universities in the U.S.[17] This constitutes an increase of eight percent over the previous academic year, and a steady increase over the past 20. Of these 106,000 scholars, 55,500 came from Asia, 31,300 from Europe, 7,000 from Latin America, 4,700 from Canada, 4,200 from the Middle East and North Africa, and 1,700 from sub-Saharan Africa. The top sending country is China with 22 percent of all visiting scholars in the U.S., followed by India, South Korea, Japan and Germany. These top five countries comprise more than 50 percent of all visiting scholars to the U.S.

The Fulbright Scholar Program, the flagship international exchange program of the U.S. government, shows a similar representation of world regions among visiting scholars, with a somewhat higher representation of scholars from the Middle East/North Africa region, Latin America and sub-Saharan Africa. The top four sending countries of Fulbright visiting scholars are China, Russia, Spain and Argentina with South Korea, the Czech Republic and Taiwan tied for fifth place. Table 3.3 compares the Fulbright scholar program with overall figures of scholar mobility to the U.S.

TABLE 3.3: SCHOLAR MOBILITY TO THE U.S. BY WORLD REGION

Visiting Scholars to the U.S.	Total	Fulbright
Asia and the Pacific	53%	46%
Europe	30%	29%
Western Hemisphere	11%	12%
Middle East/North Africa	4%	10%
Sub-Saharan Africa	2%	3%

The majority of visiting scholars to the U.S. are engaged in research (71 percent) with only 12 percent holding full-time teaching assignments and 10 percent having combined research and teaching assignments. The significant role research plays is also reflected in the top U.S. host institutions. Harvard University hosts the largest number of visiting scholars, followed by Stanford University, the University of California, Berkeley, the University of California, Davis, and Columbia University. Almost 73 percent of visiting scholars to the U.S. specialize in the STEM disciplines (Science, Technology, Engineering and Mathematics). Data from the Fulbright Scholar Program confirms the dominant role of the STEM fields. Biology, engineering and medical sciences rank among the top five academic disciplines of visiting Fulbright scholars.[18]

The continued growth of scholar mobility to the U.S. confirms the long-time leading position of U.S. universities as top research institutions and higher education destinations. Visiting scholars play an undeniable role in sustaining the leadership position of U.S. institutions, particularly in the STEM disciplines. International comparisons show U.S. students to be less prepared in mathematics and the sciences than their counterparts. For example, U.S. 15-year-olds have lower average scores in mathematics and science literacy than most of their peers from OECD member countries.[19] U.S. institutions thus welcome the inflow of well-prepared graduate students and faculty to sustain competitive research initiatives.

The influence of scholar mobility on the visiting scholars' home countries is significant as well. Research in science and technology is becoming increasingly global, as visiting scholars return to their home institutions with new disciplinary, methodological and organizational knowledge. China has had an especially deliberate strategy of using increased student and faculty mobility to the U.S. as a means of increasing the capacity and quality of its own higher education system. Scholars who studied and taught in the U.S. were expected to bring back their knowledge and experience to China with the ultimate goal of offering a top quality education to future generations of Chinese students, particularly in the STEM fields. According to Wang Yingjie, China's strategy appears to be working. The influence of the Chinese returnees is evident in stronger research programs and publication records, curricular and instructional reform, and revisions to the organizational structure of Chinese universities.

Wang writes:

A survey by the Ministry of Education in 2001 found that 51 percent of presidents of the state universities under the Ministry of Education have studied abroad. Eighty percent of the members of the Chinese Academy of Sciences and Chinese Academy of Engineering who work in these state universities have experience abroad, as do 90 percent of deans. The returnees are one of the major driving forces of reforms in Chinese higher education.[20]

And the impact of the returnees has broader implications as well. Respect for student choice and initiative was something that was virtually unknown to the more traditional teaching models customary in China. Those returning from U.S. universities had a very different educational experience. Wang writes: "…they had to be responsible for their own learning, and to exercise freedom…they learned not only facts and specific knowledge, but also the ability to think critically, from which they benefited for the rest of their lives."[21]

The impact of visiting scholars on U.S. campuses and communities is significant as well. Two case study examples from the Fulbright Scholar-in-Residence program illustrate the important role that visiting scholars play in raising awareness about other perspectives and cultures, both on and off their U.S. host campuses.

From September 2003 through June 2004, Bellevue Community College (BCC) in the State of Washington hosted its first Fulbright scholar, **Dr. Stella Williams** of the Obafemi Awolowo University in Ile-Ife, Nigeria. Dr. Williams engaged students, faculty and the community in a year-long exploration of Nigerian environmental issues and participated in various cross-cultural examinations of Nigerian fisheries and the Northwest salmon industry. Dr. Williams taught three classes including an intensive interdisciplinary seminar developed and team-taught with BCC instructors. In addition, Dr. Williams offered symposia, spoke to BCC classes and student organizations, and gave presentations at regional colleges and universities, K-12 schools and numerous civic organizations. One of her colleagues at BCC describes Dr. Williams as a beloved part of the community who "…was a role model for our students and a friend to many faculty and staff. In her outreach activities, she also supported the college's mission to be an intellectual and cultural resource for the community-at-large."[22]

The Bard Center for Environmental Policy at upstate New York's Bard College hosted Prof. **Xiangrong Wang** of Fudan University in Shanghai, China, during the 2004/2005 academic year. Dr. Wang gave several lectures and a course on "China's Strategies for Environmental Studies, Planning and Management" and provided a Chinese perspective for students and faculty at Bard. In addition, Dr. Wang lectured at the State University of New York at New Paltz, taught an upper division biology course and offered lectures to the broader New Paltz community on China's environmental issues and attitudes. His colleagues at Bard observed that studying environmental science and leaving out an important player like China is problematic. Consequently, it was tremendously valuable to host a scholar who is influential in his own country and who brought a unique perspective to two college communities, Bard and SUNY New Paltz. Dr. Wang's viewpoint often challenged that of his listeners, and the information he supplied at times contradicted what the community assumed as fact. Dr. Wang, in turn, was presented with unfamiliar viewpoints and approaches to his subject matter. Several of the U.S. students he taught reported that they planned to combine Chinese and environmental studies in their graduate work, and several faculty members have been pursuing further collaborative research.

These case study examples illustrate that the influence of visiting scholars extends far beyond their research activities. Visiting faculty enhance the learning experience of students at their U.S. host institutions and enhance the awareness of faculty colleagues and the community beyond their host campuses.

The Mobility of U.S. Scholars

U.S. scholars are among the least mobile worldwide. A 1992 Carnegie Foundation survey of faculty in 14 countries showed that U.S. faculty are considerably more insular than their non-U.S. colleagues. Survey results showed that only one-third of U.S. faculty had studied or conducted research abroad, and U.S. faculty were less likely than their counterparts overseas to view connections with scholars in other countries as very important to their professional work.

A recent study conducted by researchers at Seton Hall University does not indicate much progress during the past 15 years.[23] The study analyzes data collected in 2007 during a follow-up survey to the 1992 Carnegie study. Only 33 percent of U.S. faculty reported collaborating with international colleagues in research activities. Again, U.S. faculty ranked last among 14 countries in the percentage of articles published in a foreign country (7 percent), and among the bottom four countries in the percentage of courses taught abroad (17 percent) and the percentage of publications co-authored with foreign colleagues (5 percent).

Despite the continued comparative insularity of U.S. scholars, the 2007 survey found a significant segment that reported having integrated international perspectives into their courses, and one-third of faculty who were active in research state that they collaborate and co-publish with colleagues abroad. One of the characteristics of these internationally engaged U.S. scholars is that they themselves had international experiences during their adult years (defined as post-graduation). Faculty who spent one to two years abroad are almost twice as likely to incorporate international themes in their courses as those who spent no time abroad; and faculty members who spent more than two years abroad were nearly three times as likely to incorporate international perspectives into their courses. Faculty members who spent time abroad are also three to five times more likely to have a research agenda that is international in scope. In fact, time spent abroad proved more influential than being foreign-born or than experiencing institutional pressures to internationalize. Faculty who teach in subject areas outside of the STEM fields are also more likely to incorporate international perspectives into their courses. An increase in the presence of international students on campus, on the other hand, did not prove to be a significant predictor of the international engagement of U.S. faculty members.

Disaggregating the data into a cohort hired after 2000 and a senior faculty cohort hired prior to 2000 shows no significant differences in international engagement between the two cohorts. The assumption of the Seton Hall researchers could thus not be confirmed that "if there are dramatic changes in the extent of faculty internationalization, they would most likely be reflected among the more recent cohorts of new hires—just as these new cohorts reflect quite dramatically a greater feminization, a greater search for work-life balance, and a keen appreciation for the research pressures under which the system increasingly operates."[24] This may well reflect the lack of institutional support for the international engagement of early-career faculty members. At many U.S. institutions, pre-tenure faculty are not eligible for sabbatical leave, and international engagement is typically not considered in promotion and tenure decisions.

To some extent, the relative introspection and domestic focus of U.S. faculty are understandable. U.S. universities have enjoyed better equipment than their foreign counterparts, have provided almost unrivaled access to technology, and enjoy reliable infrastructure support. And the success of U.S. universities has been evident in the success of U.S. scholars in attaining the most prestigious international awards.[25] Yet too much introspection leads to a loss of analytical perspective, methodological diversity, epistemological breadth and innovation.

And the loss of intellectual capital associated with the limited international engagement of U.S. scholars creates a significant loss for U.S. students as well. As Table 3.2 illustrates, returned Fulbright scholars increased the international awareness of their students and colleagues, internationalized the curriculum, and arranged for study and research experiences abroad for their students.

And non-U.S. institutions lose as well. U.S. scholars have significant contributions to make in the scholarship of teaching. Education ranks consistently among the top five academic disciplines of U.S. Fulbright awards, reflecting the strong reputation of U.S. faculty in the scholarship of teaching (political science, biology, business administration and law round out the top five academic disciplines). Liberal arts college faculty are especially experienced at encouraging success among students who have traditionally had less access to higher education. For example, students from minority backgrounds enroll at independent four-year colleges at rates comparable to public institutions, yet they graduate at higher rates. For example, Hispanic students at independent four-year colleges have a 76 percent four-year graduation rate compared to 39 percent at research universities. First-generation students at private four-year colleges are more likely to succeed; their graduation rate is 61 percent versus 44 percent at public universities. Students with high financial need attend small- and mid-sized private colleges at a higher rate; smaller private four-year colleges enroll 31 percent Pell Grant recipients, public research universities enroll 24 percent.[26] The teaching expertise of U.S. faculty may be an invaluable resource for building the capacity to increase access to higher education for populations that have been marginalized in the past.

At 47 percent, Europe continues to be the main destination of U.S. Fulbright scholars. Twenty-three percent go to Asia and the Pacific, 15 percent to the Americas, 8 percent to sub-Saharan Africa and 7 percent to the Middle East/North Africa. The top five host countries of U.S. Fulbright scholars are Germany, China, Japan, India, and Ireland.

The relatively low participation of U.S. faculty in international experiences is regrettable in light of the significant positive impact international engagement has on both the scholars' home institutions in the U.S. and on their host institution overseas. Four brief case study examples of U.S. Fulbright scholars further illustrate the significant positive impact of U.S. scholars who have returned from a teaching or research experience abroad.

Brian Murphy, Professor of Fisheries at Virginia Polytechnic Institute, lectured at the Autonomous University of Guadalajara (UAG) in Mexico during the spring term of 2004. Following his return to Virginia, he arranged for a Memorandum of Understanding between his home institution and his Mexican host. The MoU provided a framework for ongoing collaborative research between PhD students and faculty at both institutions and led to the necessary permits for scientific activities in Mexico. Professor Murphy also comments in his final report that his Fulbright experience "…really helped my teaching. The serious natural resource conservation issues that I saw in Mexico spurred me to write case studies that I now use in my courses here in the USA."

Katt Lissard, Associate Professor in the Interdisciplinary Masters Program at Goddard College, Vermont, went to Lesotho in 2005 to research the theatrical response to HIV in Lesotho, which has the third-highest HIV infection rate in the world. Dr. Lissard's work at the National University of Lesotho (NUL) involved developing and producing plays with local communities about the role of gossip and silence in spreading HIV. The plays toured rural communities and proved to be an effective way to discuss the spread of HIV in a culture of silence. In addition to collaborating with colleagues at NUL, Lissard worked with visiting theater faculty from the University of Sunderland (UK) and the University of the Witwatersrand (South Africa). The multinational group founded the Winter/Summer Institute in Theatre for Development (WSI) that brings together student performers and faculty facilitators from three continents to create collaborative theater focused on HIV/AIDS prevention. The first group of students and faculty worked with rural villages in the Malealea Valley of Lesotho in 2006. Subsequently, the villagers formed their own theater group and continue to perform issue-based theater for rural mountain communities with and without WSI participation. Between residencies in Africa, WSI offers intensive weekend credit-earning workshops in New York focused on global health and community theater.

Professor **Mary E. Norton** of Felician College, New Jersey, taught Health Care Ethics at the University of Jordan beginning in 1997. Upon her return, Norton established partnerships between Felician College, the University of Jordan, and the United Nations. Her work involves students and faculty from several departments as well as international colleagues and students. Through Norton's work, Felician College was able to create a three-credit fellowship program at the United Nations and to gain official NGO status from the United Nations in 2005. Norton also established a collaboration between nursing faculty from Felician College and faculty from Case Western University, Charles Darwin University (Australia), British Columbia University (Canada) and Glasgow Caledonian University (UK) to develop a doctoral program in nursing at the University of Jordan—the first doctoral program in nursing in the region. Felician College has since signed an MoU with the University of Jordan to implement this important program.

Keith Molenaar, of the Department of Civil, Environmental, and Architectural Engineering at the University of Colorado, Boulder, received a lecturing/research grant at the Pontifical Catholic University of Chile (PCU). Molenaar conducted research at the Production Management Center at PCU, taught a course, advised students, gave seminars at neighboring universities and collaborated with faculty colleagues to improve civil engineering courses. Molenaar connected his work in Chile to the University of Colorado's Engineering in Developing Communities program that seeks to educate globally responsible students adept at developing sustainable and appropriate technology solutions. Since his return, Molenaar has worked with colleagues to create a dual doctoral degree program in engineering between the University of Colorado and PCU. Students from both universities will spend 18 months each in Chile and the U.S. and receive a PhD degree from both universities. The agreement was signed in 2008, and the first students are expected to begin their course of study this year.

These examples illustrate the tremendous contributions in research, teaching and public awareness associated with the international engagement of U.S. scholars, making the absence of such opportunities or efforts in U.S. academia all the more regrettable. What is especially unfortunate is that this lack of faculty-level internationalization has remained virtually unchanged during the past 15 years. The serious need for increased international opportunities for U.S. faculty members is particularly acute at the early careers stage where scholars have the potential of bringing significant long-term benefits to U.S. institutions, students and communities.

New Dimensions of Scholar Mobility

The world of scholars is changing. A review of the characteristics of scholarly work reveals several significant changes:

- Knowledge has become more portable in the internet age, and scholars now have access to research results and large databases from remote locations;

- Universities are no longer the sole centers of knowledge production, and research is now also conducted at research institutes, science councils and industry labs;

- More countries have developed the ability to conduct research;

- Pressing issues like climate change, water management, pandemics and global finance blur the lines between local and global inquiry;

- Knowledge networks are increasingly multinational and multidisciplinary.

These trends have implications for scholar mobility, and some of them are likely to accelerate. Stronger information and communication technology networks, for example, continue to increase access to information and to scholarly networks even from remote areas of the world. This growing access is likely to further expand the multinational and multidisciplinary character of scholarly collaboration beyond the traditional North-South links between scholars in the U.S. and Europe and colleagues in Asia, Africa, and Central and Latin America. Knowledge networks among Asian scholars, for example, already generate advances in the sciences and applied sciences that are likely to accelerate innovation and knowledge application and may shift activity away from institutions in the northern hemisphere. This trend may be supported at least in part by the research capacity of private sector facilities. There are also noteworthy examples of intergovernmental research organizations working effectively together to develop strong research infrastructures like GEANT, a high-capacity, high-speed communications network that initially connected research networks in the U.S., the EU and Japan. New research links to GEANT include China, India, Latin America, South and East Asia, North Africa, the Middle East and the Balkans.

Scholar mobility thus is becoming more multidirectional. As Thomas Friedman argues in *The World is Flat*, scholars who used to stay in the U.S. and Europe after completing their graduate work helped drive innovation and its application in the academy and the private sector. Given the improved prospects researchers now have in their countries of origin, scholars feel increasingly compelled to return to research labs and universities in their home countries. As a result, there is growing evidence that the center of gravity for scientific research and development is shifting and that the U.S. is losing its dominant position in science and technology while Asia, and to a lesser extend Europe and Australia, is gaining in importance.[27]

A World Bank report on immigration and brain drain also calls attention to the implications of this directional reversal of scholar mobility. Immigrants to countries belonging to the OECD (Organisation of Economic Co-operation and Development) are more skilled than native-born residents of OECD countries. Data for the EU show that in 2001, 23 percent of immigrants were educated at the tertiary level, compared to 19 percent of the resident population. For OECD countries these figures were 35 percent and 28 percent, respectively. As growing numbers of scholars return to their home countries, the effect will likely be a decline in the percentage of highly educated citizens residing in the U.S. and Europe.[28]

And percentages can be deceiving as well. The percentage of a population with a college degree is important, but so are sheer numbers. In 2001, India graduated almost a million more students from college than the U.S., and China graduated twice as many students and six times as many engineering majors. If future success is determined to a large extent by having the biggest and best supply of knowledge workers, the U.S. is falling behind.

The science and technology initiatives announced by the new administration of U.S. President Barack Obama are steps in the right direction.[29] The list of initiatives is long and includes a doubling of federal funding for basic research to foster home-grown innovation; increased investment in science facilities and instrumentation; increased funding to meet environmental challenges and improve global economic competitiveness; and increased funding for biomedical research, pandemics research, the physical sciences, clean energy technology, cyber security, national oceanic and atmospheric research and agricultural research.

Yet despite such new initiatives, the work ahead is challenging. The world of scholars is becoming flatter, and the international collaboration of scholars is becoming a growing factor in maintaining global competitiveness and advancing research and development. To keep pace, U.S. scholars must become far more engaged in international collaboration and adept at collaborating effectively in multinational, multicultural, multilingual and multidisciplinary environments.[30] Finkelstein and his colleagues conclude: "…what would once have been considered a mildly disturbing, but relatively harmless, bit of self-indulgence would now be considered a potentially serious disability—one with potentially far reaching consequences for the future of America's role in scientific research and development."[31]

The changing characteristics of scholarly work are accelerating the need for mobility and collaboration. For some world regions, scholar mobility will remain a vital source of capacity building and knowledge formation. For others it will become the key to maintaining access and participation in cutting-edge research, innovation and knowledge application. For the U.S., overcoming the relative isolation of its scholars will be an especially critical task that will require a substantial and sustained investment in scholar mobility. Friedman is among those who sound the alarm on the consequences of existing in a flatter world and call for diligence and fortitude—academically, politically, and economically. These academic, political and economic commitments must include significant support for research and teaching abroad in all academic fields, but most especially in those fields that drive innovation, economic development and social progress.

NOTES

[1] De Blij's "globals" are participants in the "flat world" phenomenon described by Thomas Friedman and others. Unlike some proponents of the flat world paradigm, De Blij argues that globals are the exception and that for many the world remains an exceedingly rough place.

[2] Founded in 1946, the Fulbright Scholar Program has supported the exchange of almost 250,000 scholars between the U.S. and approximately 150 countries. The Fulbright program is sponsored by the United States Department of State, Bureau of Educational and Cultural Affairs. The Council for International Exchange of Scholars (CIES), a division of the Institute of International Education (IIE), assists the Bureau in the administration of the scholar program.

[3] The persecution of scholars can also result in reduced scholar mobility as scholars are sometimes prevented from leaving their location.

[4] The Scholar Rescue Fund (SRF) is a program administered by the Institute of International Education. It provides a safe haven for scholars by placing them at universities outside of their home country. The precursor of the SRF, the Emergency Committee in Aid of Displaced Foreign Scholars, was founded in the early 1930s.

[5] Ernest Boyer, for example, suggests seven types of scholarships, all of which are associated with varying degrees of engagement in research, teaching and mentoring, and public engagement.

[6] See for example Wilson, 1979; Clark, 1987; Finkelstein, 1984 & 2007; Schuster & Finkelstein, 2006.

[7] For a discussion of globalization and the university, see for example Altbach, 2004.

[8] Universities UK, 2009, p. 3.

[9] O'Hara, 1995, p. 31. See also O'Hara, 1996 and 1999.

[10] For a recent discussion of the need for global competency, see Reimers, 2009.

[11] Green, Dao & Burris, 2008, p. 17. See also Hill & Green, 2008, pp. 30-31.

[12] Stanford Research Institute, 2002.

[13] European Commission, 2008, p. 3.

[14] Altbach & Lewis, 1996.

[15] In addition to the U.S., the study included Australia, Brazil, Chile, Germany, Hong Kong, Israel, Japan, Korea, Mexico, Russia, Sweden and the United Kingdom.

[16] The 54 countries are: Argentina, Australia, Austria, Belgium, Brazil, Bulgaria, Belarus, Canada, Chile, Columbia, Croatia, Czech Republic, Denmark, Egypt, England, Estonia, Finland, France, Germany, Greece, Hungary, India, Ireland, Israel, Italy, Japan, Latvia, Lithuania, Mexico, Netherlands, New Zealand, Northern Ireland, Norway, People's Republic of China, Poland, Portugal, Romania, Russia, Scotland, Singapore, Slovakia, Slovenia, South Africa, South Korea, Spain, Sweden, Switzerland, Taiwan, Turkey, Ukraine, United States, Uruguay, Wales, Yugoslavia (NSB, 2000).

[17] Bhandari & Chow, 2008. For the purposes of *Open Doors*, international scholars are defined as non-immigrant, non-student academics (i.e., teachers and/or researchers) at U.S. research universities. The definition does not include, for example, scholars based at the national research labs.

[18] Biological sciences, education, engineering, medical sciences, economics, and political science constitute the top academic disciplines of Fulbright scholars visiting the U.S. during the 2008-09 academic year.

[19] Bowler & Thomas, 2006. The report on the State of American Schools shows U.S. high school students' performance gaps in math and science.

[20] Wang, 2008, p. 100. Phillip Altbach has been quoted as cautioning that the impact of U.S. higher education may not be unequivocally positive, since it may result in the growing homogenization of higher education worldwide.

[21] Wang, 2008, p. 102.

[22] Final report of the Fulbright Scholar-in-Residence program, 2004.

[23] Finkelstein, Walker & Rong Chen, 2009; see also Fisher, 2009.

[24] Finkelstein, Walker & Rong Chen, 2009, p. 10.

[25] For decades U.S. institutions have also maintained a relatively high degree of diversity as scholars have visited U.S. institutions or have immigrated to the U.S.

[26] Council of Independent Colleges, 2009.

[27] See, for example, Slaughter & Rhoades, 2005; and Cummings, 2008a. See also the 2008 Hiroshima lecture delivered by W.K. Cummings.

[28] Ozden, 2006; and Eckstein, 2009.

[29] See, for example, State Science & Technology Institute, 2009; American Recovery and Reinvestment Act of 2009; and Atkinson, Castro & Ezell, 2009. To date, no explicit commitments have been made to increase scholar mobility through effective measures like the expansion of existing programs and increased collaboration between programs.

[30] The ability to collaborate rather than compete and to work in teams rather than in isolation has not been commonly valued in the academy or in higher education. Collaborative models of research may thus require a significant reorientation both at the individual and the institutional level.

[31] Finkelstein, Walker & Rong Chen, 2009, p. 2.

REFERENCES

Altbach, P. (1996). *The international academic profession: Portraits of fourteen countries.* Princeton, NJ: Carnegie Foundation for the Advancement of Teaching.

Altbach, P. (2004). Globalization and the university: Myths and realities in an unequal world. *Teritary Education and Management, 10,* 3-25.

Altbach, P., & Lewis, L. (1996). The academic profession in international perspective. In Altbach, P. (Ed), *The international academic profession: Portraits of fourteen countries.* Princeton, NJ: Carnegie Foundation for the Advancement of Teaching.

American Recovery and Reinvestment Act of 2009, H.R. 1, 111th Cong. (2009).

Atkinson, R., Castro, D., & Ezell, S. (2009). *The digital road to recovery: A stimulus plan to create jobs, boost productivity and revitalize America.* Washington, DC: The Information Technology & Innovation Foundation. Retrieved February 25, 2009, from www.itif.org/files/roadtorecovery.pdf.

Bhandari, R., & Chow, P. (2008). *Open Doors 2008: Report on International Educational Exchange.* New York: Institute of International Education.

Bowler, M., & Thomas, D. (2006, June 1). Report on the state of American schools shows high school students challenged in math and science. Press Release. Washington, DC: U.S. Department of Education. Retrieved February 25, 2009, from www.ed.gov/news/pressrelease/2006/06/06012006.html.

Boyer, E. (1990). *Scholarship reconsidered: Priorities of the professoriate.* Princeton, NJ: The Carnegie Foundation for the Advancement of Teaching.

Clark, B. (1987). Academic life: Small worlds, different worlds. Princeton, NJ: Carnegie Foundation for the Advancement of Teaching.

Commission of the European Communities. (2008). Communication from the Commissions to the Council and the European Parliament: A strategic European framework for international science and technology cooperation. COM (2008) 588. Brussels: European Commission Directorate-General for Research.

Council of Independent Colleges. (2009). Making the case: Key messages and data. Retrieved February 25, 2009, from www.cic.org/makingthecase/data/access/studentsofcolor/index.asp

Cummings, William. (2008a). *Policy-making for education reform in developing countries: Policy options and strategies*. Lanham, MD: Rowman & Littlefield Education.

Cummings, W. (2008b). The context for the changing academic profession: A survey of international indicators. In Research Institute for Higher Education (Ed.), *The changing academic profession in international comparative and quantitative perspectives. RIHE International Seminar Reports, 12*. Hiroshima, Japan: Research Institute for Higher Education, Hiroshima University.

De Blij, H. (2008). *The Power of place: Geography, destiny, and globalization's rough landscape*. New York: Oxford University Press.

Eckstein, M. (2009, January 29). Foreign-born are more likely than native-born to earn advanced degrees in the U.S. *The Chronicle of Higher Education*.

Finkelstein, M. (1984). *The American academic profession: A synthesis of social scientific inquiry since World War II*. Columbus, OH: Ohio State University Press.

Finkelstein, M., Walker, E., & Rong Chen. (2009). The internationalization of the American faculty: Where are we? What drives or deters us? [Research Paper]. South Orange, NJ: Seton Hall University.

Fisher, K. (2009, February 2). U.S. academics lag in internationalization, new paper says. *The Chronicle of Higher Education*.

Friedman, T. (2005). *The world is flat: A brief history of the twenty-first century*. New York: Farrar, Strauss and Giroux.

Green, M., Dao L., & Burris, B. (2008). *ACE: Mapping internationalization on U.S. campuses: 2008 edition*. Washington, DC: American Council on Education.

Hill, B., & Green, M. (2008). *A guide to internationalization for chief academic officers*. Washington, DC: American Council on Education (pp. 30-31).

Jarecki, H., & Kaisth, D. (2009). *Scholar rescue in the modern world*. New York, NY: Institute of International Education.

O'Hara, S. (1999). Economics, ecology and quality of life: Who evaluates? *Feminist Economics, 5:2*, 83-89.

O'Hara, S. (1996). Discursive ethics in ecosystems valuation and environmental policy. *Ecological Economics, 16:2*, 95-107.

O'Hara, S. (1995). Valuing socio-diversity. *International Journal of Social Economics, 22:5*, 31-49.

Ozden, C. (2006). Educated migrants: Is there brain waste? In Ozden, C., & Schiff, M. (Eds.) *International migration, remittances and the brain drain*. Washington, DC: The World Bank.

Reimers, F. (2009, January 30). Global competency is imperative for global success. *The Chronicle of Higher Education*.

Schuster, J., & Finkelstein, M. (2006). *The American faculty: The restructuring of academic work and careers*. Baltimore, MD: Johns Hopkins University Press.

Slaughter, S., & Rhoades, G. (2005). *Academic capitalism*. Baltimore, MD: Johns Hopkins University Press.

Stanford Research Institute. (2002). International outcome assessment of the Fulbright Scholar Program. Stanford, CA: Stanford Research Institute.

State Science & Technology Institute. (2009, January 14). S&T figures in the federal economic recovery plans. Retrieved February 25, 2009, from www.ssti.org/Digest/digest.htm

Universities UK. (2009). Researcher mobility in the European Research Area: Barriers and incentives. London: Universities UK.

Wang Y. (2008). Working with U.S. higher education: A Chinese perspective. In Laughlin, S. (Ed.), *U.S.-China educational exchange: Perspectives on a growing partnership* (pp. 99-109). New York: Institute of International Education.

Wilson, L. (1979). *American academics: Then and now*. New York: Oxford University Press.

Chapter Four

INCREASING EUROPE'S ATTRACTIVENESS FOR INTERNATIONAL STUDENTS: WHAT CAN WE LEARN FROM THE BOLOGNA PROCESS?

BY BERND WÄCHTER, ACADEMIC COOPERATION ASSOCIATION

The Bologna Process has put European higher education in the limelight. The attempt to set up the "European Higher Education Area" (EHEA), one single and coherent space of higher education, has resulted in the most comprehensive reform of European higher education structures in 30 years. As a study by Pavel Zgaga, the former Slovenian Minister of Education (and signatory of the original Bologna Declaration) displayed,[1] the reform is, in many parts of the world, regarded as a "role model." Policy-makers and academic leaders in many non-European countries have been asking themselves if they can afford not to "go Bologna." An increasing number of countries worldwide wish to formally associate themselves with the process by becoming a member. This represents a success, that Europeans did not dare to dream of when it all began 10 years ago. But it is a success mainly on a political level. This article looks for evidence of success amongst another constituency: the students. It explores the question of whether the Bologna Process has made European higher education more attractive for mobile students.

The Original Focus: Europe or the World?

It is worthwhile—and relevant for the theme of mobility—to remind the reader of the double objective that prompted the creation of the EHEA from the outset.

On the one hand, the Bologna Process was the attempt to overcome the fragmentation of Europe in terms of higher education structures. By aiming at a higher degree of "commonality"—if not outright "harmonization"—in terms of structural features, it sought to reduce barriers between countries, notably in the area of student exchange. It was thus a continuation of earlier measures started in the 1980s, such as the Erasmus Program, but a much more forceful and daring one. Erasmus and similar schemes had tried to overcome barriers posed by different educational systems by introducing complicated "conversion instruments" in the form of recognition procedures. The Bologna Process tried to do away with these barriers altogether. Both attempts, however, were staged in order to overcome system barriers *in Europe*. The aim was to create greater permeability inside the continent, and thus more student mobility.[2] In order to measure the success or failure of the Bologna reforms, one must therefore first of all look into its impact on *intra-European* mobility.

At the same time, the single European space of higher education also had global roots, and the process possessed, right from its beginning, global aspirations. One, and only one, sign of this is that the system reforms it introduced were "imports" mostly from outside of Europe. This is certainly true of the degree structure, but it also applies to credit point systems or qualification frameworks.[3] Another sign is that the EHEA was launched at a point in history when the cooperation was superseded in European higher education by a competitive paradigm. Most important of all, however, was that the Bologna Declaration clearly stated a global ambition. The EHEA had "the objective of increasing the international attractiveness of the European system of higher education"—"to ensure that the European higher education system acquires a world-wide degree of attraction."

The External Strategy of the Bologna Process

Bologna was at the outset a process that also aimed beyond Europe. But this aspect remained somewhat obscure in the first five years of Bologna's existence. The Prague Communiqué[4] of 2001 did state its goal "to promote the attractiveness of the European Higher Education Area" and stressed the need of "enhancing the attractiveness of European higher education to students from Europe *and other parts of the world* [emphasis added]." But the communiqué of the ensuing Berlin gathering in 2003 had already become much more cautious on this subject. At this time, it looked like the Bologna Process might lose its global dimension.

What came to the rescue of the "global dimension" of the EHEA? In the first place, higher education in the non-European world—after all, upwards of 90 percent of the world in population terms—started to voice its interest in the reforms and increasingly demanded some sort of association with them. Second, a number of European countries had ties beyond the continent—Spain and Portugal, for example, were linked to Latin America, and Southern Europe turned an eye to its neighbors on the African shores of the Mediterranean Sea. Third, some European networks, such as the Academic Cooperation Association (ACA), began advocacy action. In 2004, ACA staged an international conference, "Opening up to the wider world: The external dimension of the Bologna Process," which had a remarkable mobilizing effect. In the same year, the European Union started its Erasmus Mundus program, the clear aim of which is to reach out beyond the continent and attract capable postgraduate students to Europe's universities.

All of this created political momentum. At their next meeting (Bergen, Norway 2005), the ministers of education of the EHEA member states adopted a communiqué devoting considerable space to the external dimension. Most important, the communiqué stressed the need "...to elaborate and agree on a strategy for the exter-

50 | Chapter Four | Bernd Wächter

INCREASING EUROPE'S ATTRACTIVENESS FOR INTERNATIONAL STUDENTS: WHAT CAN WE LEARN FROM THE BOLOGNA PROCESS?

nal dimension." This was a turning point. At the same time, a paradoxical situation had been reached. A policy process which by its very nature aimed at the global stage found itself introducing a separate global dimension.

In the two years after the Bergen get-together, an inter-governmental working group produced the requested strategy. One of its members, Pavel Zgaga, also wrote a voluminous report on the "echoes" of Bologna in other parts of the world.[5] The strategy identified five core policy areas in which action should be taken. According to the strategy, the external dimension of the Bologna Process, which it renamed into "The European Higher Education Area in a Global Context," was to

- Improve information about the EHEA;

- Promote European higher education with the aim of enhancing its worldwide attractiveness and competitiveness (marketing of European higher education);

- Strengthen cooperation based on partnership;

- Intensify policy dialogue; and

- Further the recognition of qualifications.

The strategy constitutes a compromise typical of the Bologna Process as a whole. It balances competition-oriented elements such as marketing with cooperation-based ones like partnerships and policy dialogue. Further, it revamps existing Bologna concerns, such as the recognition of qualifications, by extending them from the European to the global stage. The strategy was adopted by Europe's education ministers at their next meeting (London 2007). The working group continues its activities, mainly by identifying needs for concrete action in the five core policy areas.

What are the chances for the strategy to be implemented? The conditions are not very favorable. The main problem is that, so far, no budget is in sight for the external dimension. It therefore appears that it will continue its existence largely on paper. The only component with some hope is the policy dialogue, but this is for rather odd reasons. In the run-up to the Leuven Ministerial Meeting (spring 2009), and in response to the urgent request of some non-EHEA countries to be more formally associated with the Bologna Process, a heated debate has developed over whether or not to create the status of a "Bologna partner" for non-EHEA countries that are already implementing Bologna-type reforms. While the European Commission favors the creation of such a status, most Bologna member countries do not. The compromise could be to replace the "status" by a looser form of association in the form of a policy dialogue.

Mobility Expectations

As stated earlier, the original hope was that the Bologna reforms would boost the international mobility of students. Exactly how they would do that was nowhere clearly stated. But the general thrust of the—largely implicit—thinking was fairly obvious. By introducing one and the same degree architecture, barriers to mobility would be reduced. By introducing ECTS, the European Credit Transfer and Accumulation System, everywhere on the continent, recognition would become easier. Qualification frameworks (a later Bologna invention) would exert a similar effect.

These expectations were all fairly simplistic. They differentiated little between different modes of mobility. They were applied to outgoing as well as incoming mobility. They were applied to intra-European mobility and mobility between the EHEA and the other parts of the world, as well as to "credit mobility" (temporary non-degree mobility in the form of exchanges) and "diploma mobility," where students moved to another country to study an entire degree program. This was naïve, to say the least.

At a later stage, from about 2005 onwards, this rather simple form of reasoning gave way to some degree of differentiation. At the same time, the discussion focused almost entirely on temporary credit-type mobility, and expectations took a radically negative turn. The conventional wisdom now was that mobility would go down, due to the shorter duration of the new bachelor's and master's degree programs, more structured (and fuller) curricula and therefore less "space" for study-abroad phases. The idea that the only way to "save" temporary mobility was to integrate mandatory phases abroad into curricula and create as many double and joint degree programs as possible became a widespread belief at this time.

The above argument has become the mainstream one, as far as temporary credit mobility is concerned. A minority of observers argued very differently but by and large came to the same conclusions. Among them is the author of this article. This group of people has drawn the attention to two issues. First, the attractiveness of a study-abroad period in Europe could be expected to wane over time. As Ulrich Teichler pointed out, temporary mobility inside Europe could be expected to have "declining currency" over time.[6] What was 20 years ago an exotic experience—to study in another European country—has today become almost banal. As research has shown repeatedly, the main impacts of study abroad are in the area of cultural and linguistic learning, as opposed to academic progress. But cultural sensitivity and foreign language command can also be acquired outside of the university—by working in another country, by falling in love with a foreign national. Second, the climate in European higher education had, over time, switched from a cooperative to a competitive mode. But the recognition of credit earned during a study abroad period rested heavily on the democratic assumption that all universities and colleges were equally good. This assumption was shared by everyone in the heydays of the early Erasmus program, with its recognition policy based "on trust." In the much more competitive days of the first decade of the new millennium, this assumption is far less likely to hold water.

With regard to intra-European degree mobility, the positive expectations have largely remained in place, although the debate about this form of mobility has never been quite as heated as the one on temporary mobility. The idea here is that the existence of one and the same degree structure across borders would make mobility from one country to another easier. One would thus see more cases than in the past of a student who studied for a bachelor's degree in, say, Portugal, went on to master's studies in Denmark and, possibly, moved to yet another country to earn a PhD.

Likewise, the belief that the Bologna reforms would attract a larger number of degree students from outside of the EHEA has survived. This expectation rested on the conviction that the structural changes, such as the new degree structure and quality assurance measures, would increase the value of European qualifications. At a first glance, this appears to be a reasonable expectation. However, it must be stressed that there is no safe knowledge yet of how the Bologna reforms impact student destination choices. A 2006 ACA study found that potential students from outside of Europe base their choice on criteria such as the perceived "reputation" of the tertiary institution, and that, anyway, they are largely unaware of the Bologna reforms.[7]

What does recent evidence tell us about the tenability of the above expectations and assumptions? What is the real effect of the Bologna reforms—inclusive of their "external dimension"—on the various forms of mobility within and into Europe? The remainder of this chapter attempts to answer these questions through a close look at empirical data. However, readers should take note that this is challenging territory and that causal relationships are difficult to establish. This is so for three main reasons:

- The Bologna reforms, and, above all, the three-cycle degree structure, are not yet fully in place in all EHEA countries. And even in those European countries where they were introduced earliest, there are at best one or two student cohorts who have fully proceeded through both the first and the second cycle. It is thus, in almost all countries of the EHEA, almost too early to measure the Bologna impact on mobility.

- As indicated above, student decisions to study in a foreign country, and destination choice, are influenced by a host of factors. It is doubtful if structural reform ranks high in this regard. But even if it did, it would be almost impossible to isolate the influence of the Bologna reforms from other factors.

- Student mobility data leave much to be desired. As will be seen further on, even attempts at improvement can sometimes be counterproductive.

Evidence I: Intra-European Non-Degree Mobility

There is no single data source that provides a Europe-wide overview of non-degree mobility. The three large international gatherers of student mobility data—UNESCO, OECD and EUROSTAT—explicitly ask their national data providers to *exclude* mobility of a duration of under one year. The standard international comparative statistics thus tell us nothing about short-term mobility at all. Some experts claim that short-term intra-European mobility is, in quantitative terms, largely identical to Erasmus mobility. This assessment appears to be based on little if any evidence. Additionally, one would expect that a share of this mobility is also generated by nationally-financed mobility programs[8] and through state-funded student loan and grants systems in some countries. The number of self-paying nondegree students not supported by any program is anyone's guess. The overview in this section, therefore, is partial at best.

Erasmus statistics show that overall numbers of grantees are still on the rise (Table 4.1). In the academic year 2006/07, there were a total of around 159,000 Erasmus grantees. Numbers have increased steadily in every single year since the creation of the scheme in 1987/88, although the most recent years have seen a strong flattening of the growth curve. Looking only at student numbers under the Socrates II program (the second phase of the EU program that aims to build "a Europe of knowledge," which lasted from 2000/01 to 2006/07), i.e. in a Bologna-relevant period,[9] numbers went up from about 111,000 to about 155,000 grantees, or by roughly 40 percent. The picture is more diverse with regard to single countries: Almost all new EU member states (who are all relatively late arrivals in the program) still show clear increases, which could be attributed to "catch-up potential." But some old EU countries have seen declines in outgoing grantees: Denmark has, over the last two years, lost about 11 percent, and Sweden went down by roughly six percent. In those countries which implemented the Bologna degree structure relatively early and in which an impact could therefore be expected, the picture is uneven: in Norway, numbers in the last available year fell by 11 percent, compared to a year before. In the Netherlands and in Italy, they were roughly stable. Of course, one must bear in mind that per capita funding in Erasmus has risen over the years, so that the incentive power of the program also increased and that numbers might be lower if that had not been so. By and large, however, Erasmus statistics provide no evidence of a decline in intra-European nondegree mobility. But they can also hardly be used to underpin the opposite assumption, that of a boost to student mobility.

TABLE 4.1: ERASMUS OUTGOING MOBILITY BY COUNTRY (ABSOLUTE NUMBERS, 2000/2001-2006/2007)

	SOCRATES II – Erasmus						
Country of home institution	2000/01	2001/02	2002/03	2003/04	2004/05	2005/06	2006/07
Austria	3,024	3,024	3,325	3,721	3,809	3,971	4,032
Belgium	4,427	4,521	4,620	4,789	4,833	4,971	5,119
Bulgaria	398	605	612	751	779	882	938
Cyprus		72	91	64	93	133	129
Czech Republic	2,001	2,533	3,002	3,589	4,178	4,725	5,079
Denmark	1,750	1,752	1,845	1,686	1,793	1,682	1,587
Estonia	255	274	304	305	444	511	572
Finland	3,286	3,291	3,402	3,951	3,932	3,851	3,773
France	17,161	18,149	19,365	20,981	21,561	22,501	22,981
Germany	15,872	16,626	18,482	20,688	22,427	23,848	23,884
Greece	1,868	1,974	2,115	2,385	2,491	2,714	2,465
Hungary	2,001	1,736	1,830	2,058	2,316	2,658	3,028
Iceland	134	147	163	221	199	194	189
Ireland	1,648	1,707	1,627	1,705	1,572	1,567	1,524
Italy	13,253	13,950	15,225	16,829	16,440	16,389	17,195
Latvia	182	209	232	308	607	681	807
Liechtenstein	18	17	7	19	26	30	44
Lithuania	624	823	1,002	1,194	1,473	1,910	2,082
Luxembourg	126	104	119	138	116	146	170
Malta	92	129	72	119	130	149	125
Netherlands	4,162	4,244	4,241	4,388	4,743	4,491	4,502
Norway	1,007	970	1,010	1,156	1,279	1,412	1257
Poland	3,691	4,323	5,419	6,276	8,390	9,974	11,219
Portugal	2,569	2,825	3,172	3,782	3,845	4,312	4,424
Romania	1,899	1,964	2,701	3,005	2,962	3,261	3,350
Slovenia	227	364	422	546	742	879	972
Slovakia	505	578	653	682	979	1,165	1,346
Spain	17,158	17,403	18,258	20,034	20,819	22,891	22,322
Sweden	2,726	2,633	2,656	2,667	2,698	2,530	2,532
Turkey					1,142	2,852	4,438
United Kingdom	9,020	8,475	7,973	7,539	7,214	7,131	7,235
Total	111,092	115,432	123,957	135,586	144,037	154,421	159,324

Source: Data provided by the European Commission, DG Education and Culture

A study titled *Transnational Mobility in Bachelor and Master Programmes*,[10] carried out by INCHER (International Centre for Higher Education Research) and GES (Association for Empirical Studies) in Kassel, Germany, in 2006, explored issues surrounding incoming and outgoing non-degree mobility in 11 European countries.[11] The study, which was produced in a very short timeframe, is based on a survey of around 200 universities and 150 bachelor's and master's programs, and thus its empirical basis is rather slim. It attempted to capture the *de facto* development of mobility in the last five years prior to the study and inquired into expectations for the future development of mobility.

Concerning the *de facto* development, 70 percent of all respondents experienced an increase in outgoing[12] non-degree mobility to European destinations, and most of the remaining 30 percent reported a stable picture. Only the Netherlands and the United Kingdom had experienced a decrease. It must be pointed out that these findings say nothing about the extent of the increase (or decrease). Respondents were not asked to provide numerical data but only to state if mobility had increased, decreased or remained stable.

However, the picture is different when one only looks at the subsample of respondents from institutions in transition from a "traditional" to a Bologna degree structure. In this group, outgoing mobility has mostly decreased or remained flat. Three percent of bachelor's programs and 4 percent of master's programs experienced an increase in outgoing mobility; 61 and 56 percent, respectively, experienced unchanged levels; and 35 and 40 percent experienced a decrease.

These findings would appear to indicate that mobility under the Bologna degree architecture is actually declining. In contrast to this, the findings concerning future expectations of outgoing mobility to European destinations in bachelor's and master's degrees point in the opposite direction. In the case of bachelor's programs, 55 percent of respondents expect an increase, 34 percent anticipate no changes, and only 10 percent expect a decrease. In master's programs, the corresponding figures are 58, 33 and 8 percent, respectively.

The German Academic Exchange Service (DAAD) carried out a questionnaire survey among some 1,600 master's and bachelor's programs (respondents) in Germany in 2006.[13] When comparing mobility between traditional degrees and bachelor's programs that had replaced them, 45 percent of respondents saw no change, 18 percent perceived an increase and 17 percent a decrease. In master's programs, 24 percent perceived unchanged mobility levels, 24 percent experienced an increase, and only 7 percent a decrease. Respondents' also predominantly expected increases in the future. As in the INCHER and GES study, the DAAD study attempted a quantitative measurement of subjective impressions ("felt mobility") and not precise data.

The latter study is particularly interesting with regard to the provisions curriculum designers in bachelor's and master's degree programs take to safeguard student mobility under the conditions of the Bologna degree structure. Twenty-one percent of all responding master's programs and 15 percent of all bachelor's programs entail a mandatory period abroad. Sixty-five percent of all programs foresee a period abroad at least as an option (which is used by between a fifth and a quarter of all students). If these German findings on the curricular integration of study abroad periods are representative of Europe as a whole, worries about a future decrease of intra-European non-degree mobility are unfounded. But it is bold to assume that the development of integrated mobility is the same in all of Europe as in Germany.

Another German study, *Internationale Mobilität im Studium*, was conducted by the Hochschul-Information System GmbH (HIS) in early 2007. Like the DAAD study cited above, it covers not only outgoing non-degree students to Europe but also non-degree students going to other continents. Both studies find that the vast majority of mobility is into Europe, but the HIS study comes to different conclusions than the DAAD survey. It is the only one which does not measure "felt mobility," but it actually surveys students and is thus based on quantitative mobility data. Master's programs have a higher share of mobility (30 percent) than some traditional "long" programs (*Diplom*/University and *Staatsexamen* 23 percent, *Diplom/Fachhochschule* 21 percent) but a lower one than others (*Magister* 34 percent). Bachelor's programs, on the other hand, have low mobility values (15 percent at universities and nine percent at Fachhochschulen). While these are interesting results, the study has a slightly unconventional methodological design and is thus not entirely comparable with the others. It surveyed students who had not yet finished their degree and thus provides only an interim snapshot of a particular stage, and, in the case of master's programs, it also counts mobility in a previous bachelor's program (and even mobility taking place between the two programs).

In conclusion, the empirical evidence for a drop in intra-European temporary mobility is slim if not nonexistent. It is, however, also impossible to conclude from these data that the Bologna degree architecture is likely to give intra-European non-degree mobility a major boost. The studies described above may also have been undertaken too early after the introduction of the new structure to draw safe conclusions. However, soon this will no longer be a major concern. In order to come to safer findings about the impact of the European Higher Education Area on intra-European mobility, it would be worthwhile to carry out a solid, country-comparative study around 2010.

Evidence II: Intra- and Into-Europe Degree Mobility

Europe has a high share of the global number of international students. The *EURO-DATA* study, which ACA carried out in 2004 and 2005 based on data for the year 2003, found slightly over 1.1 million international students in the 31 countries it covered (the now 27 EU member states, the four EFTA countries, and Turkey). This number corresponds to about 50 percent of the 2.1 million foreign students worldwide in the same year. Thus, the study found that more than half of all students worldwide studying outside their country of nationality study in Europe. In other words, at a first glance, Europe was already a strong player in international mobility in the early years of the Bologna Process.

Since 1985, when the number of foreign students in Europe amounted to roughly half a million, Europe has seen its foreign student population more than double. This impressive growth is somewhat put into perspective by the fact that total enrollment in Europe grew in the same period by about three-quarters, so that the percentage of foreign students in Europe rose only slightly, from four to five percent.[14]

Of the approximately 1.1 million foreign students enrolled in the 31 *EURO-DATA* countries in 2003, about 470,000, or 43 percent, came from the same 31 countries. About eight percent came from other European countries,[15] bringing the total share of Europeans to slightly more than half. Forty-six percent or some 510,000 were non-Europeans, and four percent of unknown origin. Of the total, the largest non-European group is made up of Asians (21 percent), followed by Africans (17 percent). North and Latin Americans make up a relatively small share, with three and four percent, respectively. The most frequent single nationality of foreign students in the *EURODATA* region was Chinese (six percent), followed by German, Greek and French (all about four percent).

FIGURE 4.1: NATIONALITIES OF FOREIGN STUDENTS IN *EURODATA* COUNTRIES

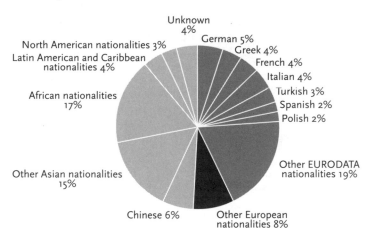

Source: EURODATA

Looking at overall European trends, two conclusions can be drawn. First, Europe is highly successful on the international "student market." Second, students from European countries make up a large share of all students in Europe studying outside their home country. This makes for a strong record in intra-European mobility, but it makes Europe's record look less impressive in terms of into-Europe mobility. Regardless, the data overstate the real extent of mobility. UNESCO, OECD and EUROSTAT have, until recently, used the foreign nationality of students as a proxy for mobility. Comparisons with data based on the criterion of "country of prior residence" and "country of prior education" in those countries that collect both showed that, in a substantial share of cases, a foreign nationality does not indicate a physical move into the country for purposes of study. In the case of some countries, the foreign student total is about one-third higher than the number of genuine mobile students. Little if any information is available on the size of the discrepancy between data on nationality and genuine mobility in other world regions outside of Europe. But the high rate of labor migration in Europe and other factors suggest that this discrepancy is higher in Europe than elsewhere in the world and that the UNESCO data therefore probably do overstate the degree of mobility in Europe, particularly the degree of intra-European mobility.

The above averages also say little about mobility with regard to single European countries. To speak of European strength in student mobility is therefore treacherous. The United Kingdom, France and Germany together account for almost two-thirds of all incoming degree mobility in Europe. Countries with a similarly large overall student population (of around two million) such as Italy, Poland and Spain have comparatively insignificant numbers and therefore much lower foreign student shares (Table 4.2).

TABLE 4.2: DOMESTIC AND FOREIGN STUDENTS IN SELECTED EUROPEAN COUNTRIES

Country	Tertiary students	Foreign students	Proportion of foreign students among all students in %
United Kingdom	2,287,833	255,233	11.2
Germany	2,242,379	240,619	10.7
France	2,119,149	221,567	10.5
Italy	1,913,352	36,137	1.9
Spain	1,840,607	53,639	2.9
Poland	1,983,360	7,617	0.4

Source: EURODATA

Likewise, the regional origin of students in Europe differs dramatically from country to country. While the share of non-Europeans reaches over 80 percent in Cyprus and Portugal, it is in the one-digit area in Slovenia and Greece.

How has mobility developed in the very recent past? Worldwide, the number of students studying outside their country of nationality has gone up tremendously, from 1.8 million in 2000, to 2.1 million in 2003 (*EURODATA* year), to 2.7 million in 2005.[16] This marks an increase of 50 percent in a period of just six years.

Table 4.3 shows, to a degree, this recent development in Europe. The data in this table have been extracted from the online database of the UNESCO Institute of Statistics, which covers the years from 2002 to 2006, i.e. a period of five years (instead of six, as in the OECD comparison). The table shows a mixed picture, with some countries making gains of close to or even over 100 percent, others experiencing a drop in numbers, and a majority registering gains between 20 and 50 percent.

TABLE 4.3: INCOMING DEGREE MOBILITY IN EUROPE (2002-2006)

Country	2002 T	2002 E	2003 T	2003 E	2004 T	2004 E	2005 T	2005 E	2006 T	2006 E	Growth T in %	Growth E in %
Austria	28,452	23,394	31,101	25,505	33,707	27,529	n.a.	n.a.	39,329	32,244	+ 38.2	+ 37.8
Belgium	40,354	24,091	41,856	22,631	26,202	7,168	21,054	11,234	24,854	13,220	− 38.4	− 45.1
Bulgaria	7,998	6,031	8,025	6,009	8,286	5,874	8,550	5,935	9,361	6,377	+ 17.0	+ 5.7
Cyprus	3,058	785	5,282	852	6,679	974	4,895	998	5,309	n.a.	+ 73.6	+ 27.1
Czech Rep	9,753	6,474	10,338	8,786	14,923	9,929	18,522	13,339	21,395	18,518	+ 119.4	+ 186.0
Denmark	14,480	6,445	18,120	7,640	9,829	7,286	10,251	7,374	12,182	8,706	− 15.9	+ 35.1
Estonia	454	436	1,090	940	830	695	884	772	1,061	793	+ 133.7	+ 81.9
Finland	6,760	3,719	7,361	4,050	7,915	4,258	8,442	4,473	11,514	n.a.	+ 70.3	+ 120.3
France	165,437	42,415	221,567	51,120	237,587	51,582	236,518	48,433	247,510	51,544	+ 49.6	+ 21.5
Germany	219,039	110,621	240,619	119,855	260,314	128,455	259,797	127,760	n.a.	n.a.	+ 18.6	+ 15.5
Greece	8,615	986	12,456	1,514	14,361	1,971	15,690	2,271	16,558	5,041	+ 92.2	+ 411.3
Hungary	11,782	9,494	12,226	9,997	12,913	10,463	13,601	11,027	14,491	11,713	+ 23.0	+ 23.4
Iceland	472	378	580	467	489	374	n.a.	n.a.	715	564	+ 51.5	+ 49.2
Ireland	9,206	4,291	10,201	4,470	12,698	4,868	12,887	4,300	12,740	4,627	+ 38.4	+ 7.8
Italy	28,447	20,611	36,137	25,781	40,641	28,539	44,921	29,841	49,090	32,644	+ 72.6	+ 58.4
Latvia	3,261	1,028	2,390	1,069	1,298	1,037	1,677	1,407	n.a.	n.a.	− 48.6	+ 36.9
Liechtenstein	n.a.	n.a.	n.a.	n.a.	412	401	n.a.	n.a.	573	538	n.a.	n.a.
Lithuania	684	252	689	299	738	420	857	520	n.a.	n.a.	+ 25.3	+ 106.3
Luxembourg	n.a.	n.a.	n.a.	n.a.	n.a.	n.a.	n.a.	n.a.	1,137	1,014	n.a.	n.a.
Malta	350	275	409	207	442	183	605	n.a.	n.a.	n.a.	+ 72.9	n.a.
Netherlands	18,874	10,775	20,531	11,814	26,154	7,434,	26,387	10,894	27,037	13,023	+ 43.2	+ 20.9
Norway	9,505	5,195	11,060	5,486	12,392	6,092	13,400	6,215	14,297	6,500	+ 50.4	+ 25.1
Poland	7,380	5,367	7,608	5,650	8,118	5,757	10,185	7,078	11,365	7,647	+ 54.0	+ 42.5
Portugal	15,692	2,797	15,483	2,809	16,155	2,874	17,010	3,034	17,077	3,173	+ 8.8	+ 13.4
Romania	10,608	8,203	9,730	7,329	10,486	7,414	10,812	7,666	8,587	5,681	− 19.1	· 59.3
Slovak Rep	1,643	1,092	1,651	1,043	1,548	1,050	1,607	1,114	1,613	1,169	− 1.8	+ 7.0
Slovenia	951	916	963	915	888	845	1,088	1,042	1,089	1,056	+ 14.5	+ 15.3
Spain	44,860	27,661	53,639	31,220	15,050	6,895	17,675	7,345	18,206	7,099	− 59.4	− 74.3
Sweden	28,664	17,211	32,469	18,786	17,253	7,475	19,966	7,872	21,315	8,254	− 25.6	− 52.0
Switzerland	29,301	23,078	32,847	25,530	35,705	27,294	36,792	28,329	28,016	19,745	− 4.4	− 14.4
United Kingdom	227,273	103,085	255,233	102,812	300,056	102,920	318,399	104,522	330,078	109,287	+ 45.2	+ 6.0

Source: UNESCO Institute of Statistics
T refers to total inbound mobility; E refers to inbound mobility from countries in Europe

Chapter Four | Bernd Wächter
INCREASING EUROPE'S ATTRACTIVENESS FOR INTERNATIONAL STUDENTS: WHAT CAN WE LEARN FROM THE BOLOGNA PROCESS?

However, there are reasons to be skeptical toward at least some of the data.

A number of countries, such as Belgium, Romania, Spain, Sweden and Switzerland, display a sudden drop of numbers from one year to the next amidst an otherwise upward-directed trend. As a result of this, their overall balance is negative. Spain, for example, drops between 2003 and 2004 from about 54,000 to 15,000 foreign students from all over the world (and from roughly 31,000 to 7,000 foreign students from Europe). This is almost certainly due to a change in the definition of a "mobile student," who was earlier understood as one with a foreign nationality and later defined as "genuinely mobile." As desirable as it is to base mobility reports on genuine mobility rather than nationality, the fact is that data measuring different phenomena now appear in a time series, limiting the usefulness of the entire series.

The increase in the case of at least one European country, Greece, where the number of foreign students from Europe skyrocketed by over 400 percent, is suspicious and probably also due to a change in statistical practice.

With a view to possible links to the implementation of the Bologna degree structure, it might be useful to look at the development of student mobility into Italy, the Netherlands and Norway, who were among the first countries to introduce the new degree architecture. The data for these three countries appear "unsuspicious." All three countries experienced gains, and increases of mobility into Europe exceed those in intra-European mobility in each country. Gains are most marked in the case of Italy (which, however, has very modest absolute numbers in relation to its size): overall mobility into the country increased by 73 percent, while mobility from Europe grew by 59 percent. Growth in the Netherlands, on the other hand, was very modest, with overall inbound mobility going up by 43 percent and mobility from Europe by 21 percent. The figures for Norway range somewhere in-between those for Italy and the Netherlands. It would, however, be misleading to attribute these developments only or mainly to the Bologna reforms. Non-degree student mobility is heavily influenced by a host of other influence factors, such as the provision of scholarship programs, visa policies (in the case of non-European students) and promotion and marketing measures.

Conclusions and Outlook

First, we have no clear evidence of the impact of the Bologna reforms on student mobility. This goes for temporary and degree mobility, and it goes for intra- and into-Europe mobility. This does not come as a surprise; it is too early to expect clear evidence. However, we do need to conduct a large-scale empirical study into the issue around 2010, when the direction of these developments will probably become clearer.

Second, if such a study found that the impact on intra-European non-degree mobility was negative, this would constitute a real blow. In the event of such a negative outcome, the author doubts that the way out should be a large increase in the number of curricula with integrated study abroad periods. These would be piecemeal solutions. The hope had been that the EHEA would be a *system*-level solution.

Third, there is much to indicate that the expectations regarding the impact of Bologna on degree mobility into the Bologna area have been overstated. This is not because the Bologna Process is the wrong kind of reform. It is so because student choice takes into account a far larger number of factors—and probably mainly others—than just structural features of higher education systems. Other internationalization measures and framework conditions play a role too: scholarships, English-medium provision, marketing, student services, international rankings, and immigration regimes, to name only a few.

Fourth, at the beginning of a very deep global recession—if not a depression—the future of study in another country, or the immediate future at any rate, is less clear than ever. If the economic downturn heavily affects the new middle classes in the big emerging economies, this will undoubtedly have a negative effect on numbers—in the Bologna zone as elsewhere.

In the longer term, the development of study abroad will depend a lot on how much progress the major emerging economies are making in domestic quality higher education provision and access. A large share of international students in the Bologna area, as in the economically advanced OECD countries in general, do not study abroad in order to have an "international" education. They study abroad to get a better education than they could have at home. If the emerging economies do catch up and improve their higher education systems, we are likely to see relative stagnation of foreign enrollments in developed countries, if not decreases.

62 | Chapter Four | Bernd Wächter

INCREASING EUROPE'S ATTRACTIVENESS FOR INTERNATIONAL STUDENTS: WHAT CAN WE LEARN FROM THE BOLOGNA PROCESS?

NOTES

[1] Zgaga, P. (2006). *Looking out: The Bologna Process in a global setting.* Oslo: Norwegian Ministry of Education and Research.

[2] It is worth noting that, given this objective, Europe did something very unusual. As my colleague Professor Ulrich Teichler pointed out, it entered into a system overhaul for the benefit of the 5 percent of international students of all enrolled students (domestic and international).

[3] Given that a good part of the Bologna agenda consists of imports, it is quite ironic that countries around the world are now considering introducing Bologna-type reforms. Many are implementing reforms based on ideas that came from them in the first place—though in a refined and systematized version.

[4] Since the adoption of the Bologna Declaration, the ministers of education of the signatory states have met every second year to review progress and to set the agenda for the following two years in the form of joint statements—the so-called communiqués. The first such meeting took place in Prague in 2001.

[5] See note 1.

[6] Teichler, U., & Janson, K. (2007). The professional value of temporary study in another European country: Employment and work of former ERASMUS students. *Journal of Studies in International Education,* 11(3-4), 486-495.

[7] European Commission. (2006). *Perceptions of European higher education in third countries.* Luxembourg: Office for Official Publications of the European Communities.

[8] One would suspect this, even though a survey conducted in the context of ACA's *EURODATA* project identified rather small numbers of these students.

[9] This sample excludes Turkey, which started to participate in Erasmus mobility only in 2004/2005.

[10] German Academic Exchange Service (DAAD). (2006). *Transnational mobility in bachelor and master programmes.* Bonn: DAAD.

[11] The 11 countries are Austria, France, Germany, Hungary, Italy, Poland, Norway, the Netherlands, Spain, Switzerland, and the United Kingdom.

[12] Like the Erasmus data, these data refer to *outgoing* mobility. In the case of intra-European non-degree mobility and with a view to possible Bologna effects, the use of outgoing student data is justified or even desirable. First, in intra-European mobility, every outgoing student is also an incoming one (elsewhere) in Europe. Second, in the event that a shorter program duration is a threat to mobility, the problem lies at the source institution and not at the receiving end.

[13] German Academic Exchange Service (DAAD). (2006). *Auslandsmobilität von Studierenden in Bachelor- und Master-Studiengängen.* Bonn: DAAD.

[14] Kelo, M., Teichler, U., & Wächter, B. (Eds.). (2006). *EURODATA – Student mobility in European higher education.* Bonn: Lemmens.

[15] These "other" European countries are mainly Eastern European states such as Russia or Belarus and countries in the South-East of the continent, in the Balkans.

[16] Organisation for Economic Co-operation and Development. (2007). *Education at a glance 2007.* Paris: OECD.

Chapter Five

JOINT AND DUAL DEGREE PROGRAMS: NEW VENTURES IN ACADEMIC MOBILITY

BY ROBERTA MAIERHOFER AND ULLA KRIEBERNEGG, UNIVERSITY OF GRAZ

Introduction

Joint and dual degree programs between two or more universities can be radical endeavors. Implementing such programs challenges institutional structures and organizational processes. It involves curricular reforms; extensive legal knowledge of local, regional, and global regulations; and strong academic involvement. It thus demands on all levels from the institutions involved flexibility, cross-cultural competence, personal and financial commitment, and a vision of the opportunities such new structures offer to the higher education community as a whole.

In 2003, a very ambitious joint degree project was launched at the University of Graz in Austria that set out to explore new forms of international academic mobility and cooperation in line with the Bologna Process. The Bologna Process, named after the Italian city of Bologna, home to Europe's oldest university, is an ambitious undertaking that was launched in 1999 when 29 European ministers of education signed the Bologna Declaration, a slim document of only about six pages that has had far-reaching consequences for Europe. It reflects the ministers' commitment to create a European Higher Education Area in order to enhance the employability and mobility of citizens and to increase the international competitiveness of European higher education. Currently, 46 European countries are engaged in restructuring their higher education systems by creating common reference points and operating procedures. Because joint degree programs call for harmonizing degree structures and quality assurance standards, they are considered important instruments for implementing the objectives set out in the Bologna Declaration. As one of the first "Joint Bologna Master's Programs" endeavors in Europe, the Graz project has been considered a forerunner in the European Higher Education Area. This article discusses the background and development of the project, while also focusing on the successes of and lessons learned by the venture.

As an integral part of the Bologna Process, the development of joint programs has in the last decade received a lot of attention from policymakers in Europe. Joint programs, in which bi- or multilateral university consortia confer joint or dual degrees to successful graduates, facilitate international academic mobility, a goal that is currently high on the agenda of European universities. Needless to say, not all of the challenges and problems that arise when trying to plan and implement joint programs among highly diverse institutions have been resolved, or even charted. Despite the ongoing structural harmonization of European systems, each university in each country still has its specific issues, and when setting out to develop a joint program, one quickly learns that the devil is in the details.

One of the first difficulties is the lack of clear terminology. While a "joint program" can mean anything from a jointly organized lecture series to a double degree program, the terms "joint and dual degree" here refer to programs that have been jointly developed by two or more universities that, upon completion, grant a dual/joint diploma—either a single piece of paper issued by all consortium members or two separate degrees. Academic degrees are granted within the legal contexts of the institutions involved, thus providing students with a diploma that is automatically accepted in all the countries of the participating universities.

In 2005, the European Ministers of Education in the Bergen Communiqué (2005) looked "for progress…in the awarding and recognition of joint degrees."[1] In the London Communiqué that was published two years later in 2007, the term "joint degrees" was replaced by "joint program,"[2] in recognition of the fact that the challenge in implementing such revolutionary new models of cooperation posed by Europe's structural diversity was greater than anticipated. This made funding available for in-between steps ("joint program") on the way to joint degrees.

Bearing in mind that the Bologna Process encompasses 46 countries from the Atlantic to the Pacific, the harmonization of educational structures and its impact on European integration and competitiveness cannot be underestimated. One common misperception, however, is that the European Higher Education Area is aiming at the development of a single undergraduate "Bologna degree," which is a three-year bachelor's degree. In reality, there are several degree structures, ranging from three-year bachelor's with two-year master's, to four-year bachelor's and one-year master's. In the United Kingdom, for example, a three-year bachelor's degree is often followed by a one-year master's. These structures vary by country and sometimes even within countries. There is no uniform "Bologna degree," but the degrees issued in Europe are supposed to be "Bologna compliant" regarding transparency, recognition, and quality assurance, and joint degrees are considered an important aspect in facilitating the goals of the Bologna Process as they require mutual understanding and adjustment of structures and systems. The Graz project can serve as an example of the successful implementation of the Bologna Process and the difficulties and challenges faced along the way.

Diversifying University Studies by Creating a Joint Vision: The "Graz Model"

When the University of Graz decided in 2003 to set up a pilot project with the aim of developing six joint master's programs in various disciplines, the concept was still rather new in the European Higher Education Area. Joint degrees had been discussed as strategic tools to reach the goals of the Bologna Process, such as increasing transparency, mobility, quality assurance, and the employability of graduates, but few had really tried to also "walk the walk" after "talking the talk."

Most consortia started with the development of professional master's programs, which, compared to research-based programs, leave more leeway in terms of legal and structural issues. Because professional master's programs are primarily employment-oriented and cater to the immediate needs of the market, they can be highly specialized and are quite flexible regarding duration and costs. As opposed to research-based or academic master's programs, which are often the results of the Bologna restructuring of formerly integrated diploma programs, professional programs do not usually qualify students for admission to doctoral studies. Thus, developing research-based programs that address the large target group of "regular students" is rather challenging. As a consequence, most consortia that decided to develop joint master's programs have opted for professional degrees because they involve less trouble with issues such as accreditation, tuition and admission than regular academic programs, which are usually subject to much stricter regulation under national laws. Another option for universities was to create highly specialized joint degrees in narrowly defined fields of research. For these reasons, very little experience was available regarding the development of research-based academic master's degree programs when the University of Graz started the pilot project in 2003, focusing on established fields of study with a broad spectrum of course options.

Despite the challenges at hand, the University of Graz nevertheless decided to develop six interdisciplinary joint master's programs. The joint master's project coordinated by the University of Graz is totally in line with the Bologna accords, sharing the following characteristics:

- The programs are research-based master's programs in line with the Bologna accords (120 European Credit Transfer and Accumulation System-credits, two years).

- The study programs, curricula, admission and examination regulations are jointly developed and recognized by all consortium partners while respecting the individual universities' conditions.

- Students spend part of their studies (minimum 30 ECTS credits, one semester) at another partner institution. This part, as well as all examinations completed at a partner institution, is fully and automatically recognized at a student's home institution.

- The courses offered are taken from the already existing programs of the participating universities. No new courses need to be developed. Each university contributes to the program its own field of expertise.

- Summer schools serve as "catch-up classes" or bridge courses that count towards the 30 ECTS credit requirement of the mobility phase.

- Upon successful completion of the study program, students receive one joint diploma which is issued and recognized by all partner institutions.[3]

The University of Graz decided to launch such an ambitious project as one of the university management's priorities for the following reasons that all correspond to priorities set by the Bologna declaration: Joint programs increase the crosscultural competencies of students, faculty, and staff, not only by encouraging international mobility but also by enhancing internationalization at home. The introduction of interdisciplinary high-quality programs was seen as a chance to position the University of Graz in the region. In addition to facilitating the implementation of Bologna goals, which has been declared a strategic focus by the university management, the project also contributed to strengthening the second focus area, cooperation with South-Eastern Europe. Based on its longstanding collaboration with higher education institutions in this region, Graz was the first university in the German-speaking countries to establish a focus on cooperation with South-Eastern Europe as a profile-setting feature of its university developmental concept. One of the aims of this strategy is to involve the countries of South-Eastern Europe in the creation of a common European Higher Education Area. Joint degree programs are perfect vehicles to do so, as a high degree of international mobility, transparency, and joint quality assurance mechanisms is involved. Thus, the high quality of joint academic programs is guaranteed, which again contributes to a broader and more intensive understanding of the highly diverse models of European universities. Last but not least, students with international and crosscultural experience who, in addition to their language skills hold international degrees, seem to have competitive advantages in the labor market, as a study carried out in 2008 by the European University Association (EUA) showed.[4]

By securing financial support through the local government it was possible to offer incentives to the initially somewhat hesitant university community. One of the main tasks was to explain and lobby at all levels of the university, in order to explain the structure and the benefits of such a study program. A lot of time was spent in meetings, where informational material was distributed and members of the senate and the curricula committees were persuaded of the added value of joint degree programs. In a second bid, the project was extended to include further interdisciplinary master's programs and one doctoral program. Funding was secured for developing a summer school, providing additional scholarships and making it possible to hire staff for the increased administrative efforts necessary to coordinate more than 20 institutions from Europe, the U.S. and Asia. Adding new partners and organizing activities such as cooperation meetings and small conferences, summer schools, and presentation of the project at international conferences required additional commitments from the University of Graz. Today, two experts in the Office for International Relations coordinate the development and implementation of the programs on the administrative level in cooperation with the Vice Rector for International Relations and Interdisciplinary Cooperation. The academic issues are the responsibility of professors working in the field of the joint programs. In order to advance the university's competitive profile, the joint degree project became a strategic focus area with special support from the rectorate.

Name of the degree program	Consortium members
M.A. in English and American Studies	- Graz / Austria - Paris 7, Denis Diderot / France - Bamberg / Germany - Pécs / Hungary - Ca'Foscari Venice / Italy - The City College of the City University New York / U.S.A. - (Roehampton / United Kingdom: associated partner)
M.A. in Jewish Studies – History of the Culture of the Jews	- Graz / Austria - College for Jewish Studies Heidelberg / Germany
M.A. in History of South Eastern Europe	- Graz / Austria - Cluj / Romania - Ljubljana / Slovenia
M.Sc. in Sustainable Development	- Graz / Austria - Leipzig / Germany - Ca'Foscari Venice / Italy - Hiroshima / Japan - Utrecht / The Netherlands - Basel / Switzerland
M.A. in Gender Studies	- Graz / Austria - Bochum / Germany
M.A. in Latin American Studies	- Graz / Austria - Leuven / Belgium - Poitiers / France
M.Sc.. in Cultural Sociology	- Graz / Austria - Zadar / Croatia
PhD in Diversity Management and Governance	- Graz / Austria - Sofia / Bulgaria - Bologna / Italy - Primorska / Slovenia

Issues in Joint Degree Development

In the course of this project, many lessons were learned. At the onset, little was known about joint degrees, and therefore the joint degree team decided to act as a facilitator for future projects by passing on their experience to colleagues and at international conferences, such as the EAIE conferences (European Association of International Educators) in Krakow, Poland (2005), Basel, Switzerland (2006) and others, by presenting information on the homepage, and by making themselves available for consulting. Although there is no such thing as a generic recipe for joint degree development, some of the issues and challenges were recurrent. The following paragraphs summarize the main problems: coordination; curriculum design/length of programs; finding a common language; tuition fees and funding; mobility; and issuing a joint diploma. In our discussion of these challenges, we use the joint degree project in English and American Studies as an example.[5]

Coordination

As the University of Graz is currently coordinating one large umbrella project with more than 20 partner universities in eight research-based joint degree programs, the level of structural complexity is quite high. What proved enormously important right from the beginning was the fact that there was sufficient funding available already for the coordination and development phase. Actually, almost half of the project budget went into staff and travel expenses. Only about one quarter was earmarked for student and teacher mobility for the second phase of the project. This way, international consortium meetings could be held without overburdening the partner universities' budgets—a fact that should not be underestimated. Yet, it was decided to ask the partner universities for at least some financial support, e.g. when sending their delegates to meetings. This proved important, as it ensured that the partner university's management had been informed about the project and, most importantly, demonstrated the partner's commitment. As a first step, a letter of intent was signed, which was the basis of all further steps. Although these letters did not involve legal obligations, they proved that the university was committed to developing such a joint degree, regardless of how the implementation procedures were defined after the completion of the curriculum development.

While the University of Graz provided the administrative support, the partner institutions nominated an academic coordinator who attended the meetings, determined the academic content and kept university management informed about the progress of the project. What proved most important was the flow of communication among all coordinators. With an international consortium, communication is not an easy task because the issues and difficulties increase (ideally in proportion to the added value) with each partner university. It involves detailed knowledge of all partners' structural and academic issues as well as of the highly diverse legal systems that apply. Not all universities are autonomous regarding curriculum development, tuition, and the granting of degrees. Sometimes, regional laws or national laws need to be considered. Most importantly, however, the flow of information within every single partner university needs to be facilitated in order to avoid unpleasant surprises at later stages of development. Management changes also need to be taken into account: even minor changes in university administration bear risks and require intensified communication efforts—which cost extra time and effort. Therefore, the most important strategy to ensure sustainability of a project is involving as many people as possible at an early stage. If the project is linked to only one person, the consortium might risk losing a partner if this person leaves the project.

Curriculum Design / Length of Programs

Whereas the Bologna Process introduced a three-cycle-system (bachelor's, master's, and PhD) in the whole of Europe (and beyond), the length of each individual cycle has been decided within individual national contexts. Thus, you will find 3+2 systems and 4+1 systems (bachelor's and master's programs) within the European context and also, in the case of British universities, a 3+1 system. In the case of the specific degree described, Roehampton University in the UK needed to introduce this two-year master's program, as all their other master's degree programs are only one-year-programs. Therefore, Roehampton University currently holds the status of an associated partner, while the university moves forward in the process of becoming a full member.

Regarding structural differences in curriculum design, such as non-European grading schemes, for example, U.S. universities have proven far more flexible than their European counterparts. The modular system of the curriculum was designed to accommodate the U.S. university's needs, which was easier than expected due to the way U.S. universities function in terms of program development and independence. A conversion table for ECTS grades and U.S. grades was added to the cooperation contract, the second key document in addition to the curriculum. This way the consortium managed to also incorporate universities that are not using ECTS credits.

It was more difficult on the level of academic contents to find a common denominator for each consortium. The "Tuning Project,"[6] an EU-funded project that was started in the year 2000 to harmonize European educational structures with emphasis on the subject area level that is the content of studies, provided excellent advice regarding curriculum modularization. After a first consortium meeting of the program coordinators for English and American Studies where it seemed almost impossible to reconcile six different curricula, a modular structure with a clear emphasis on learning outcomes instead of detailed academic contents emerged as the perfect solution to accommodate each partner's needs.

As these examples show, a good knowledge of legal requirements and structural procedures was necessary in order to reconcile the very different needs of the seven partner institutions. Sometimes, university management had to adapt statutes or bylaws, including passages referring to joint degree programs. More importantly, however, the consortium members worked on the basic assumption that all involved universities served high standards in teaching and research, had good quality assurance mechanisms in place, and operated on a sophisticated level concerning regulations and procedures. Having chosen the partner institutions carefully, the negotiations were conducted on the basis of mutual trust, and joint regulations were kept to a minimum. As a rule, the respective regulations of each individual university guarantee a high standard in teaching and research. In addition, however, joint quality assurance mechanisms were developed, and accreditation processes required by partner institutions (for example in the case of German universities) by European agencies such as ACQUIN[7] and AQAS[8] were set up as part of the program.

In this project, effort was made to establish such a program based on existing courses. The consortium members decided that the added value would be a larger variety of courses students could choose from and a range of dedicated professors with diverse areas of research who could act as their teachers and advisors.

Finding a Common Language

When trying to construct a common curriculum or negotiate a cooperation contract, it is important for everybody involved to have a reasonable working knowledge of any common language. Especially when negotiating nitty-gritty details, this is indispensable in order to avoid misunderstandings and conflict. The muddle of terminology aside, there are still plenty of traps apart from linguistic misunderstandings that can lead to a lack of program coherence. Usually, the working language of an international consortium will be English. Most of the time, this is the only solution when working with international partners who do not share a common official language, even if it is far from perfect. Even if all delegates present at a meeting are able to speak a common language other than English, it cannot be assumed that everybody who will deal with the curriculum and cooperation contract at a later stage is able to read additional foreign languages. Some universities may require translations of all relevant documents into their official language.

Especially when working with countries with strict language policies such as Slovenia, Belgium or France, language issues can be of great relevance. In Slovenia, for example, national law requires that courses offered in English must also be offered in Slovene (unless they are language classes). Only up to 10 percent of all courses offered at a university can be in a foreign language. This means that students who spend their semester at a Slovene partner university either have to be fluent in Slovene or, if the university offers courses taught in English, these courses might have to be doubled in Slovene—which impacts the university budget.

The language aspect was taken into consideration when the idea to develop joint degrees at the University of Graz was put into practice. For exactly this reason, Graz chose to start with the joint degree in English and American Studies. It could be assumed that academics working in this field had perfect language skills, which already eliminated one of the obstacles, the lack of a common working language. The idea proved successful. The negotiations actually started with a meeting of vice-presidents and professors, who were also scholars of English and American Studies. The original plan was to set up a program that focused on a central European perspective on the scholarly field of English and American Studies. In order to pay tribute to the university network in the context of which the idea had been generated, in its beginning phase it was called "English and American Studies for the Alps Adriatic Region." Apart from the advantages of developing a degree in the framework of an established university network, a regional focus was considered highly relevant for the development of a regional identity within the context of the European Union.

Tuition Fees and Funding

One of the most sensitive issues in joint program development is the question of tuition fees. In contrast to professional master's degrees, research-based programs in some European countries cannot charge cost-covering fees or determine joint tuition for such a program. Most European universities—with the exception of British institutions—charge relatively small fees, due to culturally different approaches to higher education access. In the case of the Graz project, it was not possible to determine a standardized fee for all students due to individual universities' regulations. Therefore, tuition fees are charged by the home university. Students in their mobility phase are regarded as regular students and are granted normal access to the facilities of the host university. Local fees and health insurance provisions may vary by institution.

The aspect of tuition has been a longstanding and controversial topic in Europe. Especially since the introduction of Erasmus Mundus,[9] a program of the European Commission with the aim of enhancing mobility and cooperation within joint programs between universities in Europe and beyond ("third countries"), the issue of tuition fees has been hotly debated. Erasmus Mundus requires an agreement on joint tuition and registration fees. It does not take into account that some universities may be legally bound by national or other legislation and cannot independently agree on charging tuition. Recently, Erasmus Mundus has made provisions to solve this problem by allowing the consortia to determine the distribution of a consortium's income, which is not always an easy undertaking, especially when the solution involves unequal distribution. This funding policy of the European Union has influence on the structure of joint degree programs and transatlantic cooperation. Although in the European Union policy responsibilities regarding education are officially still in the hands of individual member states as regulated in the Treaty of Maastricht (European Union 1992), the European Commission has a strong influence on the implementation of the Bologna reforms and the creation of a European Higher Education Area that reaches far beyond the borders of the European Union. A major stakeholder and sponsor of cooperation programs, the European Union affects national higher education agendas and, by means of the Bologna Process, has become a major player in the global field of higher education.

Mobility

Encouraging international academic mobility has been a major policy goal in the European Higher Education Area. From 1987 on, the Erasmus[10] program has grown to be the largest program in the world supporting temporary study abroad. With the introduction of Erasmus Mundus in 2001, enhancing the attractiveness of the European Higher Education Area for students from other parts of the world became a priority. This rationale had already been prevalent in the U.S., Canada, Australia, and the United Kingdom for a number of years but found its entry to continental Europe only with the Bologna Declaration and the European Council's Lisbon Conclusions (2000) that formulate as a strategic goal of the European Union "to become the most competitive and dynamic knowledge-based economy in the world, capable of sustainable economic growth with more and better jobs and greater social cohesion."[11] Clearly, higher education policy is seen as a vehicle to facilitate European integration and economic competitiveness. Thus, joint program development, which as a core aspect includes international academic mobility, ties in perfectly with the educational, political, and economic rationales of the European Union.

Regarding the Graz project, student and teacher mobility are integral parts of the programs. It is a requirement of a two-year joint master's program that at least 30 ECTS credits (one semester course work) be acquired at an institution other than the home institution. Ideally, the stay abroad would be in the second or third (out of four) semesters. For administrative reasons, the first semester is to be spent at the home institution. Already when applying for admission to the program, students are asked to indicate their preference concerning the universities for their study abroad stay. If possible, these preferences will be taken into consideration by the coordinators. Some places, however, especially those at U.S. universities, are allocated on a competitive basis, in order to acknowledge the different funding systems. This allows for U.S. universities to balance the number of incoming and outgoing students. Within the European context, mobility programs such as Erasmus cover at least part of the costs. Special scholarships have been established for U.S. students at the University of Graz in order to offer additional incentives to participate in such a program.

Credit transfer and recognition are integral parts of a joint degree program. A detailed learning agreement is negotiated between student and program coordinator (academic advisor) in order to ensure that the student take advantage of all available opportunities to the greatest possible extent. In case a student is unable to acquire 30 ECTS credits during his or her mobility phase, an additional summer school, "GUSS- Graz University Summer School,"[12] offered in cooperation with the partner institutions, can be used as a catch-up course and counts towards a student's mobility credit requirements. The summer school consists of a balanced mixture of seminars in the topic areas in the morning, transferable skills workshops in the afternoon, meet-the-professor sessions in the evening, as well as various cultural events such as excursions. In addition, it facilitates networking for students and teachers, leads to stronger teaching and research collaboration among partner universities, and provides intercultural learning in a more relaxed atmosphere. Again, extra funding is provided by the University of Graz and the European Commission to cover costs for student and faculty mobility.

Issuing a Joint Diploma

As a recent report released by the Institute of International Education (IIE) and Freie Universität Berlin shows, most joint programs are double degree programs.[13] Upon completion of the program, a student in this case receives two diplomas, usually issued by the institutions where credits were acquired. These diplomas are recognized officially in the countries where the degree-awarding institutions are located. If a consortium consists of many partners, a multiple degree is also possible. The Graz project consortia decided to issue joint diplomas instead of double/multiple diplomas, providing students with one diploma signed by all consortium members. Needless to say, there are many questions that need to be addressed, among them language policies, data transfer and data protection, document design, safety regulations, and awarding procedures. Also, the way in which a diploma is awarded can vary significantly between cultures. To meet the requirements of all universities involved, a diploma design workshop was organized in order to find a common denominator.

Apart from the question of which information a diploma needs to include, one of the biggest problems with joint degrees is the assumption that a student can only obtain a degree from a university where he or she has spent at least a certain proportion, often more than 50 percent, of his or her time. In a consortium with more than two member universities, this regulation can no longer be applied. The universities need to agree that having studied a joint curriculum, a student can receive a joint diploma. As with many other aspects of joint program development, mutual trust in combination with accurate quality assurance and official program accreditation are key components of joint degree development.

Lessons Learned and Still Being Learned

Because each joint program has its own specifics and local contexts, it is very difficult to come up with general guidelines of how to develop joint programs that would be of help to new consortia. Many of the issues have already been mentioned above. One of the standard guidelines worth mentioning, however, is the European University Association's 10 "Golden Rules for New Joint Masters' Programmes."[14] Despite the rather general nature of this document, the checklist proved extremely helpful in the planning and implementation phase of a joint or double degree program.

In addition, our experience showed that it is absolutely vital for the success of a project that commitment is ensured not only on the academic and administrative levels but also that university leadership is involved. A project with such high complexity needs to be organized in both a top-down as well as a bottom-up fashion. If the university management is convinced that a joint degree program in a certain field is desirable but the faculty in the field do not fully support the idea, the project will most probably fail because its success depends to a large extent on personal commitment and networks at the academic level. If, on the other hand, academics or administrators support the project but the university management is not committed on all levels, from department heads to deans and the rectorate, the project will fail as well— not least due to a lack of financial support.

Furthermore, sustainability of the program needs to be considered. In the U.S., sustainability is harder to attain than in many European institutions. The high degree of independence of U.S. universities and their market-orientation makes them move very fast, and their flexibility makes the implementation of new structures fairly easy.

On the other hand, it bears the risk of change when project partners change or key figures and their commitments are lost.

Last, but not least, European universities can learn a lot from their U.S. counterparts in terms of public relations. In Europe, competition among universities is still a rather new development and its possibilities have not yet been fully explored. Advertising a program and attracting as many (international) students as possible is of great importance, especially when each student enrolled at an institution is counted and leads to an increase in funding for the institution. The University of Graz decided to provide public relations materials for each consortium, including a website, posters, and folders, using a corporate design. All partner institutions are supplied with these materials. The production and dissemination costs of such materials can be kept at a reasonable rate, and they enable the project coordinator to keep track of all changes, avoiding confusion and misinformation.

Conclusion

Joint degree programs not only contribute to transparency and harmonization of structures in European and transatlantic higher education cooperation but also facilitate mobility of students and faculty. Generations of students remember the complications of translating grading schemes, explaining transcripts, and arguing with their advisors back home for their course work to be accepted at their home institutions. They would have wished for automatic recognition of credits earned during their study abroad period. Joint degree programs include this feature as a built-in mechanism and can be considered new and radical ventures in academic mobility.

This article argues that such programs are radical endeavors for various reasons. The Graz joint degree project described in this article is unique in its approach to educational cooperation at the level of joint research-based master's degrees, because only very few programs confer actual joint diplomas on this level. The University of Graz and its partner institutions have set a goal to increase the quality of their academic programs by contributing to the diversity of courses offered, gaining a competitive edge on the labor market for graduates of these programs by awarding joint degrees.

Coordinating several joint programs not only contributes to a university's international reputation but also creates a global network of administrators, scholars and students who share common goals. It facilitates international mobility and advances the implementation of Bologna goals. It increases campus internationalization and crosscultural awareness. Despite the challenges such an attempt involves, the joint degree projects described in this article have always been considered worthwhile undertakings by everybody involved.

NOTES

[1] Norwegian Secretariat of the Bologna Follow-up Group. (2005). *Bergen Communiqué – The European Higher Education Area – achieving the goals. Communiqué of the Conference of European Ministers Responsible for Higher Education, Bergen, 19-20 May 2005.* Bologna-Bergen 2005, p. 5. Retrieved December 22, 2008, from www.bologna-bergen2005.no/Docs/00-Main_doc/050520_Bergen_Communique.pdf

[2] Benelux Bologna Secretariat. (2007). *London Communiqué – Towards the European Higher Education Area: Responding to challenges in a globalised world.* Retrieved January 11, 2009, from www.ond.vlaanderen.be/hogeronderwijs/bologna/documents/MDC/London_Communique18May2007.pdf

[3] For further information please also refer to the project website at www.jointdegree.eu

[4] Timofei, A. (2008). Developing and implementing joint programmes in Europe: The results of an EUA study. In Froment, E. et al. (Eds.), *EUA Bologna handbook: Making Bologna work* (Vol. 9, C 4.5-4, p. 17). Berlin: Raabe.

[5] For reasons of clarity, the following paragraphs refer to the program in English and American Studies as an example. This program has the largest consortium with seven partner universities including a U.S. partner (the City College of the City University New York) and has served as a model for the other projects. One person was involved both on the academic level as professor of American Studies as well as on the management level as Vice Rector for International Relations in charge of the Graz Joint Degree Project, which made it possible to monitor all steps involved.

[6] European Commission – Education and Training. (2008). *Tuning educational structures in Europe.* Retrieved December 23, 2008, from http://ec.europa.eu/education/policies/educ/tuning/tuning_en.html

[7] ACQUIN – Accreditation, Certification and Quality Assurance Institute. Retrieved January 15, 2009, from www.acquin.org/en/index.php

[8] AQAS – Agentur fuer Qualtitaetssicherung durch Akkreditierung von Studiengaengen (Agency for quality assurance through accreditation of degree programs). Retrieved January 15, 2009, from www.aqas.de

[9] European Commission – Directorate General for Education and Training. External relations programmes: Academic mobility with Erasmus Mundus. Retrieved January 11, 2009, from http://ec.europa.eu/education/external-relation-programmes/doc72_en.htm

[10] European Commission – Directorate General for Education and Training. Erasmus for higher education. Retrieved January 11, 2009, from http://ec.europa.eu/education/lifelong-learning-programme/doc80_en.htm

[11] European Council. Presidency Conclusions: Lisbon European Council 23 and 24 March 2000. European Parliament. Retrieved January 30, 2009, from www.europarl.europa.eu/summits/lis1_en.htm

[12] University of Graz – Office of International Relations. GUSS – Graz University Summer School. Retrieved January 15, 2009, from www.jointdegree.eu/?id=96&lng=1

[13] Institute of International Education and Freie Universität Berlin. (2009). *Joint and double degree programs in the transatlantic context: A survey report.* New York: IIE, p. 5. Retrieved January 28, 2009, from www.iienetwork.org/?p=TDP

[14] European University Association. (2004). *Developing joint masters' programmes for Europe: Results of the Joint Masters Project (March 2002 – January 2004)*, pp. 23-24. Brussels: European University Association. Retrieved January 11, 2009 from www.eua.be/eua/jsp/en/upload/Joint_Masters_report.1087219975578.pdf

Chapter Six

HIGHER EDUCATION RANKINGS AND THE GLOBAL "BATTLE FOR TALENT"

BY ELLEN HAZELKORN, DUBLIN INSTITUTE OF TECHNOLOGY

> ...[T]he government is very keen for Australia's export image to be seen to have these high class universities and then...say to the world look we have high class universities in Australia, come and study here. You don't only have to go to the U.S. or the UK...[it is a question]...of the export image.

> The government wants a first class university for international prestige...Rankings are becoming important to present Japan attractively and getting good students and good workers as the population declines. That's the government's motivation. [1]

The Global Battle for Talent

A few years ago, few people outside of the U.S. were familiar with the ranking of higher education institutions (HEIs). Today, global rankings or cross-national comparisons have emerged as an inevitable by-product of globalization and international competitiveness. As internationalization has become a priority for both government and higher education, the talent-catching and knowledge-producing capacity of higher education has become a vital sign of a country's capacity to participate in world science and the global economy. Student mobility is one of the main forms of internationalization and, according to the OECD, countries with high levels of international students benefit from the contribution they make to domestic research and development, while those with low numbers find it "more difficult...to capitalize on this external contribution to domestic human capital production."[2]

The positioning of knowledge as the foundation of economic, social and political power has been driven by the transformation of economies based on productivity and efficiency to those based on higher-valued goods and services developed as a result of innovation and talent. If the first phase of globalization was marked by "working cheaper," the current phase is measured by connecting people and processes globally and breaking down traditional barriers.[3] Almost 80 percent of a company's value comes from intangibles or soft knowledge—unique knowledge of services, markets, relationships, reputation, and brand.[4] Successful economies are those which rely more on the ability to exploit knowledge for "competitive advantage and performance...through investment in knowledge-based and intellectual assets: R&D, software, design new process innovation, and human and organizational capital."[5] The EU Lisbon Agenda, which aims to make Europe "the most dynamic and competitive knowledge-based economy in the world" by significantly increasing investment in R&D to 3 percent GDP and doubling the number of PhD students,[6] is a prime example of this "talent-dependent" strategy.

Ironically, this approach has emerged at a time when many OECD countries are facing demographic challenges. This has arisen for a combination of reasons, including graying of the population and retirement of professionals combined with the end of the "baby boomer" bubble and decline in the number of students, especially those choosing science and technology subjects. In the U.S., the pool of high school students is anticipated to fall by 10 percent over the next decade, and colleges and universities risk being closed down or merging with competitor institutions.[7] The number of 18-year-old Japanese has fallen from 2.05 million in 1992 to 1.3 million in 2007 and is likely to drop to 1.21 million by 2009. The German government predicts that even with 200,000 immigrants a year, Germany's population will shrink from today's 82.5 to 75 million by 2050; the number of students matriculating from undergraduate to graduate study has shrunk so much that restrictions on the number of students, which had been introduced to maintain very high standards, had to be lifted.

As a result, what Japan's *Daily Yomiuri* calls the "scramble for students" and the *Economist* refers to as the "battle for brainpower" has moved center stage, complementing more traditional struggles for natural resources. Knowing that people with higher levels of education are more likely to migrate,[8] governments around the world are introducing new policies and targeting high-skilled immigration—especially in science and technology—to attract "the most talented migrants who have the most to contribute economically."[9] The importance of mobility stems not just from its contribution to the production and dissemination of codified knowledge but also from transmitting tacit knowledge in the broadest sense. There can be benefits for both sending and receiving countries (not just brain drain but brain circulation), if the latter has the appropriate absorptive capacities to attract (back) and retain high-skilled talent.[10] Internationalization, once seen simply as a policy of cultural exchange, is increasingly viewed as a necessary mechanism to increase the number of international students, especially graduate (PhD) research students.

The importance of the lucrative international student market has raised the global competitive stakes. In terms of actual numbers and percentage of total students, Western Europe and North America are the world regions of choice. Together, they host approximately 1.7 million of the 2.5 million international students, or 70 percent of all international students.[11] Under GATS, international or cross-border student mobility has become a recognizable, tradable commodity that is likely to encompass 7.2 million students annually by 2025.[12] But this is not a simple good news story for receiving regions and their economies. While the number of receiving countries is growing, countries that have traditionally sent students abroad are quickly expanding their domestic HE capacity. UK universities have been urged to "buckle up for a rough ride" while Japanese universities are having to "send…recruiters out to high schools, hold…open houses for prospective students, build…swimming pools and revamp…libraries, and recruit…more foreign students."[13] As a counter measure, governments are seeking better alignment between higher education, innovation and immigration policies to guarantee access to the global talent pool.

The remainder of this chapter will look at the impact that rankings of HEIs have on student choice and mobility and the way in which both HEIs and government are responding to global competition for talent. It draws on the results of an international survey of HE leaders in 2006 and interviews with HEIs in Australia, Japan and Germany during 2008. The research was conducted under the auspices of the OECD Programme for Institutional Management of Higher Education, the International Association of Universities, and the Institute of Higher Education Policy—the latter with funding from the Lumina Foundation. There are three main sections: *Part 1* describes the growing importance that rankings are having on student mobility and student choice; *Part 2* provides an overview of the recruitment and other initiatives HEIs are adopting; and *Part 3* looks at policy reaction. The final section offers some concluding observations on the way in which rankings are accelerating competition for the lucrative international student market.

Rankings and the Global Higher Education Market

While rankings have become very popular in recent years, they have existed—in the U.S.—for a long time. *U.S. News and World Report (USNWR)* began providing consumer-type college-guide information for students and their parents in 1983. The demand for more comparative information, and greater accountability and transparency has intensified ever since. Today, national rankings exist in over 40 countries. Global rankings are recent but they are also more influential; the Shanghai Jiao Tong *Academic Ranking of World Universities* (henceforth SJT) began in 2003, followed by *Webometrics* and Times QS *World University Ranking* in 2004, the Taiwan *Performance Ranking of Scientific Papers for Research Universities* in 2007, and *USNWR's World's Best Colleges and Universities* in 2008. The EU has announced a "new multi-dimensional university ranking system with global outreach" to be piloted in 2010. Rankings' popularity has risen for the following two reasons:[14]

1) Because higher education is now seen as the motor of the economy, global rankings are perceived as providing a gauge of international competitiveness as measured by the number of a given country's HEIs in the top 20, 50 or 100. Politicians often refer to them as an expression of national ambition, and their results are covered widely in the popular press. HEIs widely believe that rankings enable them to build, maintain or elevate their reputation and profile (nationally and internationally); that

high-achieving students use rankings to shortlist institutional choices, especially at the graduate level; that stakeholders use rankings to influence their decisions about funding, sponsorship and employee recruitment; and that high rankings bring benefits and advantages. A high rank is seen as self-perpetuating once achieved, but there are also down-sides: "by far and away the most important is reputational risk."[15] In other words, on a year-to-year comparison, a lower ranking would be perceived as a decline in standards and quality.

2) Because graduate and employment outcomes are strongly correlated with higher qualifications and institutional type,[16] students (and their parents) have become savvy consumers. Institutional reputation is a key driver of student choice, and much of the attractiveness of rankings is their simple, easy-to-understand format. They provide a fast, short-hand Q-mark, enabling the user to "pre-sort" a group of HEIs prior to more in-depth inquiry.[17] They are also an attribute of self-pride and peer-esteem. There are positive vibes associated with a high ranked HEI, while students in low ranked institutions fear the reverse may be true. Thus, in the UK, 61 percent of students referred to rankings before making their choice, and 70 percent considered them important/very important,[18] while 60 percent of prospective German students "know rankings and use rankings as one source of information among others."[19] Forty percent of U.S. students use news magazine rankings, and 11 percent report that rankings are an important factor influencing their choice.[20]

Students are not a homogeneous group, and their attitude towards the use of rankings can be divided into, at least, four distinct groups.

- *Domestic undergraduate students* usually attend a local university, but depending upon circumstances and choice, this could be within their city or a geographically adjacent region. As such, they are likely to use a combination of local intelligence, local rankings or entry scores—the more difficult a university is to enter, the better it is seen to be. There is growing evidence that high-achievers are becoming more mobile, and HEIs are beginning to target this group with special packages. For the bulk of domestic students, ranking consciousness rises while at university, usually because of internal communications from the president, faculty, brochures or conversations with peers.

- *International undergraduate students* represent a proportion of the total student cohort that varies depending on the country of destination.[21] Full-time international students make their choice based on family or institutional connections, although ease of residency and employment opportunities, in addition to access to higher education, are also factors. For students who may spend a portion of their undergraduate studies abroad, their decisions are often made on the basis of institutional partnerships, albeit within the choice available, some students do consider reputational factors.

- *Domestic graduate students* are likely to have become conscious of rankings while at university and use them to inform their graduate choice. While they do make more complex choices based on their field of specialization and expertise of faculty, they are keenly attuned to the perceived after-sale value of their qualification. High-achieving graduate students are increasingly likely to travel either within their country or to another country. Indeed, the idea of remaining at the same institution for undergraduate and graduate studies is increasingly frowned-upon.

- *International graduate students* are the major users of global rankings—not least because there is often less information available locally to them than to students in major host countries. A recent UK study confirmed that 92 percent of international students considered UK league tables important/very important to inform their choice.[22] Because the majority of international students fund their studies from their own/family sources, rankings fulfill an important function. They are likely to "choose the country and subject areas of the study" based on their calculations regarding the monetary and status reward a foreign degree can bring.[23] Thus, they "might know about Australia, but not where in Australia to go." Institutional rank transmits social and cultural capital, which resonates with family, friends and potential employers.

This is particularly critical for students seeking employment in their home country—but it can work both ways. As one student said:

> ...I have a colleague who graduated from Columbia University and she's holding a very high position....They did not tell me frankly but I could read their minds that if I am lucky enough to graduate at this university I could not be as highly appreciated as the one who graduated from Columbia University.

Cross-border mobility within particular regions is also growing; students in Arab countries migrate to Egypt and Jordan, and students from Bangladesh and Nepal travel to India for opportunities not readily available at home.[24]

There are other differences. Students seeking employment in some professions such as business, medicine, law or academia appear more sensitive to institutional status than other students. This is because the former subjects have a history of being ranked, while for others, employment opportunities in the academy are often influenced by the reputation of the institutions from which the qualifications have been acquired.[25]

But students of different abilities and socioeconomic backgrounds also make different kinds of choices. Research in the U.S. has found that rankings are particularly significant for high-ability and second-generation students, especially students from Asian backgrounds.[26] Richard Spies argues that above-average students make choices based on non-financial factors, such as reputation.[27] Students who have the financial ability to pay full fees and are not reliant on government or other grants—who are effectively free to choose—are more likely to attend higher ranked colleges (even by a few places) than grant-aided students who appear to be less responsive to rankings. Clarke also cites UK, German and New Zealand experiences that high-achieving students are more likely to use rankings to inform choice. Research indicates an increase in the use of rankings among lower-income groups,[28] but responsiveness among elite students and parents remains most significant.[29]

Attendance at the most select universities and colleges is seen to "confer extra economic advantages to students, in the form of higher early career earnings and higher probabilities of being admitted to the best graduate and professional schools," albeit this may be more for "under-represented minority students and students from low-income families."[30] It also confers indirect benefits, such as connections to "elites" and future decision-makers, membership of "the right" social and golf clubs and schools, etc. Accordingly, there is growing evidence that students have "tried to increase the standing of their program in satisfaction-based rankings by sending back surprisingly upbeat surveys."[31]

Not enough is known about the influence of the media and public opinion, but it is clear that students are sensitive to media coverage and publicity. One administrator stated: "The *Good University Guide* doesn't influence student recruitment but media reporting of it does" while another commented that "one university…suffered a very steep drop in enrollments internationally and it's because of bad publicity.…" A student similarly observed:

> …people have a general perception, an accepted perception of which university is the best and which is second best and third best and so on. It's just out there among the community. Even worldwide people know that Harvard, Oxford and Yale and Cambridge are like the top universities because they see and hear it in movies and all the different culture and media and that really establishes people['s] perception of them.…People automatically see the name of the university…in all these little articles and they get it drummed into their head that this university must be at the cutting edge, it must be at the forefront and it's obviously respected by people if it keeps showing up with different things.…

In summary, undergraduate students are relatively less influenced by rankings than graduate students, who comprise the fastest growing number of internationally mobile students worldwide.[32] The latter are more responsive to worldwide rankings given their maturity, career focus and capacity for mobility, in addition to increasing national and institutional anxiety and efforts to recruit these lucrative students who can also shore up national research and economic development strategies.

Rankings and Student Recruitment

In this context, it is not surprising that competition between countries and HEIs for (top) students is rising. While the U.S. has had lengthier exposure to disseminating information about its higher education system and to rankings, international experience is converging. HEIs use rankings to inform strategic decision-making, aid branding and enhance visibility nationally and internationally:

> …those who are looking at their institution on an international scale are fully aware of the potential of these ratings, rankings, evaluations to attract students, to attract faculty and so on and it is also commented in…the newspapers, in comments in the media and so on….

While some HEIs vie for high rank, for many others just being mentioned can be beneficial, helping to overcome local bias or tradition.[33]

> Since global rankings have appeared, we are receiving an increasing number of foreign delegations.

> Our "profile has increased because of rankings" among international students, recruitment agencies and other HEIs who want to form partnerships with us.

Effectively "caught between not wanting to place public emphasis on their ranking…and privately trying to avoid slipping,"[34] HEIs are compelled to respond to the growing presence of rankings and specifically the way in which rankings have raised the competitive bar. As a result, they are making changes across their organizations.

Although there is no evidence that lower ranked universities lose students, students can and do modify their behavior in response to rankings, and a high ranking does lead to increased applications,[35] causing perceptible "ebbs and flows in the number and quality of applicants,"[36] especially among international students. An institution whose rank improves also has greater scope for enhancing its position. It can accept a smaller percentage of its applicants and thereby enhance its selectivity index, a metric used by *USNWR* and *The Sunday Times*. On the other hand,

> …a less favorable rank leads an institution to accept a greater percentage of its applicants, [leading to] a smaller percentage of its admitted applicants [who] matriculate, and the resulting entering class is of lower quality, as measured by its average SAT [college entry] scores.[37]

And the circle repeats itself, leading to a downward spiral in terms of ranking position. Because difficulty of gaining entry is often interpreted as higher quality, HEIs often seek to influence the number of applicants they receives while still retaining the actual number of available places. Hence,

> …[t]oo many institutions now spend their resources aggressively recruiting students with high SAT or ACT scores and other conventional markers of achievement that correlate strongly with socioeconomic status. In turn, at many institutions those choices skew the allocation of financial aid from students with the great need to those with the most offers of admission.[38]

These actions may encourage HEIs to abandon distinctive missions—such as widening access or diversity—that are not measured in rankings.

While selectivity indices have not been a significant element of other national or worldwide rankings, especially in Europe where equity and open recruitment has tended to be the norm, there is evidence of change. Even in systems, such as in Ireland, where student admissions are effectively "blind" to subjective factors, there are suggestions HEIs have endeavored to influence the process for similar reasons indicated above. At the graduate level there is less secrecy: HEIs use rankings to assess the suitability of applicants' undergraduate experience, especially international students, "so we're as guilty."

Private institutions are better able to respond to ranking pressure, given their ability to use endowment funds or adjust tuition fees to influence "student input" metrics used by some ranking organizations, such as *USNWR*, but this pattern is growing also. Other methods include using scholarship or merit aid to "purchase talent" or invest in "image-enhancing face lifts," such as dormitories, fiber optic networks and sports facilities.

HEIs are improving, refocusing or developing admissions policies and procedures, and expanding their marketing and publicity activities into year-round professional offices with rapidly expanding budgets and staff. Many are heavily involved in student and trade fairs in key countries. Admissions and international officers confirm that prospective students regularly inquire as to institutional rank. Almost 50 percent of international respondents and 35 percent of U.S. HEI presidents use their rank for publicity purposes,[39] highlighting (positive) results on their webpage, in speeches, at new faculty or student orientations or international meetings, or when lobbying government. A notable number even advertise on the webpage of the ranking organizations.

For particular professional disciplines such as business, rankings are perceived/used as equivalent to professional accreditation. Despite differences, both systems 1) measure number of graduates and professors, research output, etc., 2) bring international recognition, and 3) are used by prospective students to identify a good place to study. Professional accreditation enhances mobility, opening doors to future employment. While there is some disagreement about whether professional accreditations influence the ranking of a particular institution, their absence could be a stumbling block. Conversely, professional bodies are influenced by rankings, and this could in turn influence the outcome of the professional accreditation process.

International recruitment is having a significant and long-lasting impact on language diversity, because to be successful requires transforming programs and activities into English—even when, as in Japan for example, over 92 percent of foreign students come from Asia, of which 60 percent are Chinese and 15 percent Korean. Most Japanese universities are focusing on post-graduate activities, initially in science and technology fields where they already have a reputation likely to be attractive to international students:

> So it's obvious that some departments will introduce English not in the social science or the international relations but in engineering...if we could teach these courses in English then recruiting international faculty would be easier.

New facilities are also required: new and more dormitories, world-class labs, and international student services and amenities, in addition to recruitment of international scholars, often at attractive salaries. But this may not be enough. One student was asked why she went to Japan rather than to an English-speaking country with better quality education and a lot of high ranking universities.

Policy Responses

High skilled mobility is shaped by a combination of push and pull factors. While general migration has strong economic incentives, high skilled mobility responds to more complex factors, including educational and professional development, research opportunities, work conditions, access to infrastructure and quality-of-life features such as participatory recreation, culture and outdoor recreation, and societal diversity. Escalating global competition and demographic changes have compelled governments to introduce an array of new policies with respect to international students, with special emphasis on high-achieving students and graduates.[40]

Vital to this strategy is the prestige, reputation and attractiveness of the higher education system, individual HEIs and qualifications. In the absence of other cross-national comparative information, global rankings have acquired a prominence beyond their original intent, and are now perceived and used as a quality mark and indicator of value-for-money of the entire higher education system. Top ranking HEIs "act as magnets for the brightest students from countries unable to provide world-class standard tertiary education."[41] National competitions, for example the UK Research Assessment Exercise or the German *Exzellenzinitiative* (see below), have acquired a similar status, used by students and other stakeholders. One institution, unsuccessful in the first round of the latter competition, was asked: "Are you not excellent anymore?" Thus, despite criticism of the methodologies used by the various ranking organizations, governments and government agencies are aware of the potential of these ratings to attract students and faculty.

Global rankings can be decisive for students seeking government sponsorship/scholarship to study abroad (e.g., scholarships in Mongolia and Qatar are restricted to students admitted to highly ranked international universities)[42] or recognition of foreign qualifications (Macedonia automatically recognizes qualifications from the top 500 universities listed in the Times Higher Education Supplement (THES) or SJT or USNWR).[43] In a move likely to be repeated by other governments, the Dutch are using rankings to approve skilled migrants, but only if they graduated from a university in the top 150 of the 2007 SJT or the Times QS Rankings.[44]

Many governments are going further. Two main policy regimes are emerging:[45]

1) *Create greater vertical (reputational) differentiation [neo-liberal model]:*
Germany, Japan, China, Korea, and France are using rankings as a free market mechanism, driving the concentration of "excellence" in a small number of research-intensive universities. Part of the aim is to attract high-performing research-intensive students and faculty and ward off demographic challenges in the future. For example, Germany fears a "shortage" of domestic students after 2015 and therefore sees international recruitment as vital. The German *Exzellenzinitiative* (2005) aims to create a German "Ivy League" that can compete successfully in world science and boost international visibility, giving "a little more glamour to Germany" by increasing interest from international students and faculty who are finding it is "not as easy as…before to get a visa to the U.S.," and also from employers and industrial partners. Similarly, Japan aims to increase the number of international students from its current 100,000 to 300,000 by 2020. The "Strategic Fund for Establishing International Headquarters in Universities"[46] (2005) aims to create an internationally competitive research environment that will attract outstanding researchers from within Japan and abroad.

2) *Create greater horizontal (mission) differentiation [social-democratic]:*
Australia wants to "brand Australia" with a horizontally "diverse set of high performing, globally-focused HEIs." A similar approach has been adopted by Norway. Rather than elevating a small number of elite institutions to world-class status, the recent Australian Review of Higher Education seeks to build a world class HE system providing excellence across diverse fields of learning and discovery, impacting economic and social development.[47] In contrast to an emphasis on competition as a driver of excellence (as the above example), the focus here is recognizing and rewarding excellence wherever it occurs as a way to underpin social and regional equity. The Norwegian Commission for Higher Education, reporting in January 2008, takes a similar approach to its structural and competitive challenges. Rather than opting to concentrate investment, it recommended building up "excellence wherever it occurs."[48] In a different way, the University of Catalonia brings together eight different universities under a single umbrella to maximize capability beyond individual capacity.[49]

Public policy in the U.S. differs across the different states. According to Eckel (2008), the characteristics of low government intervention, diverse funding and mission-based accreditation are being supplanted by increasing focus on the role of higher education as a driver of economic growth and innovation. This policy shift is creating a more competitive "market-driven environment [which] favors prestige" factors[50] such as rankings as a mechanism of differentiation. In this respect, the neo-liberal experience referenced above reflects the U.S. experience.

In either case, governments around the world are busy restructuring higher education in order to improve productivity and efficiencies, support national policy objectives and enhance the world-class status and reputation of the system. This involves merging and/or strengthening HEIs by building a critical mass of active researchers in specialist fields winning more competitive funds and producing more verifiable outputs, with national/international partners. Directly or indirectly, the goal is to improve ranking position.

Conclusion

Rankings have risen in popularity because they are perceived to provide an independent assessment of the performance of higher education. As qualifications have become mobile and higher education viewed as the driver of the economy, global rankings have acquired significance far beyond their original intention. In the absence of other cross-national comparative information, they are interpreted by students and others as a mark of quality—and effectively, their ability to attract international students is a measure of that quality. Today, internationalization is less about cultural exchange and more about economic survival.

> The danger of not responding adequately to the challenge of internationalization is tremendous as the best academic institutions are competing intensely to attract the best talent.[51]

Thus, global rankings are the realization that in a global knowledge economy, national pre-eminence is no longer sufficient.

In teaching and research, national boundaries are declining in significance, and world-wide comparisons will be more significant in the future. This has implications even for "elite" HEIs, which may have been dominant within their national boundaries but are now compelled—like their regional colleagues—to operate in a "single world market." All HEIs, globally oriented and regionally focused, have been drawn into the global market. Institutions and countries that can maximize their attractiveness to high-achieving students and highly skilled labor succeed. Accordingly, HEIs are choosing not just to benchmark themselves against peers in other countries but also to forge consortia through which research, program development, student and faculty exchange, and recruitment occurs, creating global higher education networks. New and different types of rankings and comparative directories will emerge.

At a time when demographic changes are shrinking the number of (traditional) students and intensifying competition, rankings help build brand awareness. Despite criticism and cynicism, few HEIs can afford to ignore their influence. While cost may be less important for top-ranked universities whose "appeal derives from their continued scarcity and prestige as positional goods, and the perceived social networks they may offer,"[52] rising fees and more competition will make students (and their parents) more focused on value-for-money and quality.[53] This is likely to put a cap on the extent to which countries use international students as financial fodder—and put more power into the hands of students. In order to be successful, countries and HEIs will need to adopt different strategies if they are to win their share of the global talent pool.

[1] Unattributed quotations are from participants in an international survey of higher education leaders in 2006 and from interviews with higher education institutions in Australia, Japan and Germany in 2008. Both studies are described on page 81. Participants were guaranteed anonymity given the sensitivity of the issues involved. No reference is given to country or institutional type except in a general way.

[2] Organisation for Economic Co-operation and Development. (2007). *Education at a glance* (p. 34). Paris: OECD.

[3] Cheese, P., Thomas, R.J., & Craig, E. (2007). *The talent powered organization: Strategies for globalization, talent management and high performance.* London: Kogan Page. Retrieved January 5, 2009, from www.accenture.com/NR/rdonlyres/9ADBFE69-938C-4388-833C-CC8502305C85/0/TPOChapterOne.pdf

[4] Hutton, W. (2006). Building successful cities in the knowledge economy: The role of 'soft policy' instruments. Retrieved January 8, 2009, from www.oecd.org/dataoecd/11/22/40077480.pdf

[5] Brinkley, I. (2008). *The knowledge economy: How knowledge is reshaping the economic life of nations.* London: The Work Foundation (pp. 17-18). Retrieved January 3, 2009, from www.workfoundation.com/assets/docs/publications/41_KE_life_of_nations.pdf

[6] Retrieved February 19, 2009, from http://europa.eu/scadplus/glossary/research_and_development_en.htm

[7] Marcus, J. (2008, July 3). The state of the union. *Times Higher Education.*

[8] Eurobarometer. (2006). *Europeans and mobility: First results of a EU-wide survey on geographic and labour market mobility* (Fig. 1). Retrieved January 3, 2009, from http://ec.europa.eu/employment_social/workersmobility_2006/uploaded_files/documents/FIRST%20RESULTS_Web%20version_06.02.06.pdf.

[9] Rüdiger, K. (2008). *Towards a global labour market? Globalisation and the knowledge economy* (p. 5). London: The Work Foundation. Retrieved January 8, 2009, from www.workfoundation.com/assets/docs/publications/30_globalisation.pdf

[10] Hvistendahl, M. (2008, December 19). China entices its scholars to come home. *Chronicle of Higher Education.*

[11] Guruz, K. (2008). *Higher education and international student mobility in the global knowledge economy* (p. 230). Albany, NY: SUNY Press.

[12] Varghese, N. V. (2008). *Globalization of higher education and cross-border student mobility* (p. 11). Paris: International Institute for Educational Planning, UNESCO.

[13] McNeill, D. (2008, July 11). Facing enrolment crisis, Japanese universities fight to attract students. *Chronicle of Higher Education;* Gill, J. (2008, July 10). Buckle up for a rough ride, UUK tells sector. *Times Higher Education.*

[14] Hazelkorn, E. (2008). Learning to live with league tables and ranking: The experience of institutional leaders. *Higher Education Policy 21:2,* 195-215, and (2007). The impact of league tables and rankings systems on higher education decision-making. *Higher Education Management and Policy, OECD, 19:2,* 87-110.

[15] Unattributed quotations used come directly from the above-mentioned study. Anonymity was promised to all respondents.

[16] Santiago, P., Tremblay, K., Basri, E., & Arnal, E. (2008). *Tertiary education for the knowledge society, vol. 2. Equity, innovation, labour market, internationalisation.* Paris: OECD. (pp. 189-233).

[17] Contreras, A. (2007, July 31). The cult of speed. *Inside Higher Education.* Retrieved January 3, 2009, from www.insidehighered.com/views/2007/07/31/contreras

[18] Roberts, D., & Thompson, L. (2007). University league tables and the impact on student recruitment, reputation management for universities – Working Paper Series No. 2 (p. 20). Leeds, Cambridge and Brisbane:

The Knowledge Partnership. Retrieved January 3, 2009. from www.theknowledgepartnership.com/docsandpdf/leaguetablepressrelease.pdf

[19] Federkeil, G. (2007). Rankings and quality assurance in higher education, presentation to 3rd meeting of the International Ranking Expert Group (IREG 3), Shanghai.

[20] McDonough, P. M., Antonio, A.L., Walpole, M., & Pérez, L.X. (1998). College rankings: Democratized college knowledge for whom? *Research in Higher Education, 39:5*, 513-537.

[21] Organisation for Economic Co-operation and Development. (2008). *Education at a glance* (p. 358). Paris: OECD.

[22] Roberts, D., & Thompson, L. (2007). University league tables and the impact on student recruitment. Reputation management for universities – Working Paper Series No. 2 (pp. 5, 18-20). Leeds, Cambridge and Brisbane: The Knowledge Partnership. Retrieved January 29, 2009, from www.theknowledgepartnership.com/docsandpdf/leaguetablefinalreport.pdf

[23] Varghese, Op Cit., p. 22.

[24] Ibid. p. 23.

[25] Wedlin, L. (2006). *Ranking business schools: Forming fields, identities and boundaries in international management education.* Cheltenham, UK: Edward Elgar; Sauder, M., & Lancaster, R. (2006). Do rankings matter? The effects of U.S. News & World Report rankings on the admissions process of law shools. *Law & Society Review, 40:1*, 105-134; Berger, M. (2001). Why the USNWR law school rankings are both useful and important. *Journal of Legal Education, 51:4*, 487-502.

[26] Griffith, A., & Rask, K. (2007). The influence of the USNWR collegiate rankings on the matriculation decision of high-ability students: 1995-2004. *Economics of Education Review, 26:2*, 244-255; Ehrenberg, R. G. (2001). Reaching for the brass ring: How the USNWR rankings shape the competitive environment in U.S. higher education. Paper prepared for Macalester Forum on Higher Education; Monks, J., & Ehrenberg, R.G. (1999). *U.S. News & World Report's* College Rankings: Why they do matter. *Change, 31:6*, 43-51.

[27] Spies, R. R. (1978). *The effect of rising costs on college choice: A study of the application decisions of high-ability students.* Princeton, NJ: College Board Publication Orders.

[28] McManus quoted in Roberts, Op Cit., p. 18.

[29] Machung, A. (1998). Playing the rankings game. *Change, 30:4*, 12-16.

[30] Ehrenberg, R. G. (2004). Econometric studies of higher education. *Journal of Econometrics, 121*, 19-37.

[31] Clarke, M. (2007). The impact of higher education rankings on student access, choice and opportunity. In IHEP (ed.), *College and university ranking systems: Global perspectives and American challenges.* Washington, DC: Institute for Higher Education Policy, pp. 35-47; Coughlan, S. (2008, July 25). Faculty in league table expulsion. *BBC News.* Retrieved January 5, 2009, from http://news.bbc.co.uk/2/hi/uk_news/education/7526061.stm?TB_iframe=true&height=650&width=850

[32] Guruz, Op Cit., pp. 172-175.

[33] Hazelkorn (2007), Op. Cit, Figure 5.

[34] Griffith and Rask, Op. Cit.

[35] Monks and Ehrenberg, Op. Cit; Ehrenberg (2001), Op. Cit., pp. 2, 10.

[36] Dichev, I. (2001). News or noise? Estimating the noise in the U.S. News university rankings. *Research in Higher Education ,42*, 238.

[37] Monks and Ehrenberg, Op. Cit.

[38] Lovett, C. (2005, January 21). The perils of pursuing prestige. *Chronicle of Higher Education.*

[39] Hazelkorn (2007), Op. Cit.; Levin, D. (2002). The uses and abuses of rankings. *Association of Governing Boards Priorities Magazine, 20.*

[40] Varghese, Op. Cit., pp. 22-25, and Santiago, Op. Cit., chapter 10.

[41] Santiago, Op. Cit., p. 25.

[42] Salmi, J., & Saroyan, A. (2007). League tables as policy instruments: Uses and misuses. *Higher Education Management and Policy, 19:2*, 52.

[43] Macedonia: Article 159 of the Law on Higher Education, February 26, 2008, number 35/2008.

[44] Beerkens E. (2009, January 6). What if I graduated from Amherst or ENS de Lyon…. Message posted to http://blog.beerkens.info; Beerkens E. (2008, July 1). On the use of rankings and league tables. Message posted to http://blog.beerkens.info/index.php/2008/07/on-the-use-of-rankings-and-league-tables

[45] Hazelkorn, E. (2009). Rankings and the battle for world class excellence: Institutional strategies and policy choices. *Higher Education Management and Policy, 21:1*. Forthcoming.

[46] www.jsps.go.jp/english/e-quart/13/index02.html

[47] Australian Government Department of Education, Employment and Workplace Relations. (2008). *Review of Australian higher education.* Canberra, Australia: Commonwealth of Australia. Retrieved February 19, 2009, from www.deewr.gov.au/he_review_finalreport

[48] Norwegian Commission for Higher Education, http://stjernoe.no/site/in-english

[49] www.acup.cat/index.php?option=com_content&task=view&id=77&Itemid=137

[50] Eckel, P. (2008). Mission diversity and the tension between prestige and effectiveness: An overview of US higher education. *Higher Education Policy, 21*,188.

[51] Universitat Politècnica de Catalunya. (2008). *From international relations to internationalisation. International policy plan, 2008-2015* (p. 4). Retrieved January 8, 2009, from https://www.upc.edu/sri/strategy

[52] Lee, J., Maldonado-Maldonado, A., & Rhoades, G. (2006). The political economy of international student flows: Patterns, ideas, and propositions. In Smart, J. (Ed.). *Higher education: Handbook of theory and research, 21*, pp. 545-590 quoted in Santiago, Op Cit, p. 249.

[53] Marcus, Op. Cit.

Chapter Seven

GLOBAL COMPETITIVENESS IN SCIENCE AND TECHNOLOGY AND THE ROLE OF MOBILITY

BY TITUS GALAMA AND JAMES HOSEK, RAND CORPORATION

Introduction

Policy and decision makers across the globe view science and technology (S&T) as crucial to a nation's ability to develop economically, improve the well being of its people, and strengthen its national security. Many nations, including those that excel in S&T and those that do not, have concerns about the performance of their S&T enterprise, their S&T infrastructure, and the quantity and quality of their science and engineering (S&E) graduates and S&E workforce.

Developed nations perceive a growing ability of developing nations to compete in knowledge-intensive sectors that once were believed to be relatively immune to outsourcing (buying services from foreign suppliers) and offshoring (shifting work to foreign locations). The factors driving their concerns include the globalization of S&T, the rise of science centers in countries such as China and India, and, in the U.S., lagging student performance on international math and science achievement tests. Although the U.S. is currently the undisputed leader in S&T, it must recognize the growing capacity in other regions in light of their increasing world share in publications, citations and patents and of the growing number of S&E graduates in China, India, and Europe at a time when U.S. students appear to be less interested in pursuing S&E studies than studies in business, medicine, and law. The European Union (EU) is concerned about falling further behind the U.S. because of the brain drain to the U.S., the high contribution of research and development (R&D) expenditures from the U.S. private sector compared with those in the EU, and the growing S&T capacity in developing nations such as China, India and South Korea. Developing nations such as South Korea in turn have made significant strides in S&T but feel pressure from more recent players such as China and India. Traditional mid-income countries such as Mexico already find themselves overtaken by a number of developing nations in S&T capability despite having made investments in S&T at a much earlier stage (Silberglitt et al., 2006).

The importance of S&T to the future of these nations is reflected in their commitment to public initiatives to develop their S&T capability. In January 2006, China initiated a 15-year "Medium- to Long-Term Plan for the Development of Science and Technology." China aims to become an "innovation-oriented society" by 2020 and a world leader in S&T by 2050. In March 2000, the EU heads of state agreed to make the EU "the most competitive and dynamic knowledge-based economy in the world" by 2010—the so-called Lisbon Strategy (Euractiv, 2004). Two years later, the EU set a goal to increase its average research investment level from 1.9 percent to 3 percent of GDP by 2010, of which two-thirds should be funded by the private sector as compared with 56 percent in 2002. These demanding goals may not be reached, but the agreement over the goals underscores the widespread consensus that S&T are fundamental to securing a nation's economic future. Ambitious programs are not limited to large players such as China and the EU. Many small nations and regions are competing with one another to attract and build knowledge-based industries. The efforts of Singapore, Wallonia (Belgium) and Ireland in building biotechnology clusters are just a few of many such examples.

S&T are highly knowledge-intensive, so it is no surprise that human capital is a most essential ingredient to a well-oiled S&E enterprise. S&E workers are highly mobile compared to workers in professions that require similar levels of education, such as medicine and law. An engineer can begin work in the U.S. or Europe immediately following his/her graduation from one of the Indian Institutes of Technology (IITs). The same cannot be said for recent graduates in medicine or law, who may need to be trained and certified according to U.S. or European standards and practices in those fields. The international migration of scientists and engineers is limited more by the availability of work permits than by the transferability of skills and knowledge. Even language is arguably less of a barrier than it used to be, as English has become the common language of science (Montgomery, 2004).[1]

Our work in this field began with an assessment of U.S. competitiveness in S&T (Galama & Hosek, 2007a) in response to numerous public and private sector reports appearing in the mid-2000s that argued that the U.S. is falling behind in S&T and that gave rise to a wave of legislation on Capitol Hill. We examined the claims that U.S. S&T was faltering, drawing upon relevant data including historic trends and international comparisons in research and development investment; in the size, composition, and pay of the U.S. S&E workforce; and in domestic and international education statistics. We found that the U.S. continues to lead the world in S&T and has kept pace or grown faster than other nations on several measurements of S&T performance; that it generally benefits from the influx of foreign S&E students and workers; and that it will continue to benefit from new technologies, even those developed by other nations, as long as it maintains the capability to acquire and implement such technologies. We concluded by recognizing that the U.S. leadership in S&T should not be taken for granted, however, as the globalization of S&T is a powerful force of change with ultimately uncertain outcomes. In Galama and Hosek (2007b) we provide recommendations to strengthen the U.S. S&E enterprise, including measures to facilitate the immigration of highly skilled labor and improve the U.S. education system.

In this chapter we build on this work by updating the comparisons in our previous study with newly released data, by taking a more international perspective, and finally by extending our discussion to include further consideration of the risks and gains to mobility to both the receiving and sending nations. One can obtain a general picture of a nation's S&T prowess by piecing together information from several quantitative indicators, as long as various indicators are not in huge disagreement with one another. Given the complexity of the problem, economists and policymakers cannot determine the "right" amount of effort and investment in S&T for a nation; at a minimum, we can compare a nation's current investment with its historic investment to learn whether its investment is increasing or decreasing, and with other nations to learn how much they have chosen to invest and with what results. Throughout this chapter we make such historic and international comparisons to draw conclusions on the performance of nations in S&T and their investment in S&T infrastructure, education and the S&E workforce.

We first describe the changing nature of innovation and the rise of developing nations in S&T and discuss the potential implications of these trends for both developed and developing nations. We then focus on the crucial role of migration of S&E talent to the success of nations in S&T. From past research on migration within the U.S. it was known that the rate of migration from one part of the country to another increases with the level of education, with the highest rate at the highest level of education. This has meant that the market for highly educated workers is national, i.e., job search is national and wages are in effect equilibrated nationally. Building from this, the ongoing prosperity of the U.S. as well as the globalization of economic activity has provided incentives for the market for highly educated workers to become global. This has impelled bright individuals everywhere to follow economic opportunity, leaving their home country for jobs in the U.S. and graduate study in the U.S. that opens doors leading to jobs. The U.S. position is not unique, however; the same insights apply to other countries. EU countries are attractive to many workers, and the formation of the EU paved the way to considerable migration between EU countries. Similarly, the economic rise of Korea, China, and India has created a demand for highly educated workers within those countries, and workers have sought higher education and have in many cases relocated to where the best jobs are offered in their country and sometimes abroad. We do not expect these trends in the demand for highly skilled workers to abate, and, as we discuss, we find reason to believe that global competition for college-educated workers will intensify in the future as a result of demographic trends. At the end of the chapter we briefly summarize the discussion and conclude.

The Rise of Other Nations: Research and Development Efforts Worldwide

Globalization is changing R&D from a national endeavor supported largely with public funds and to a lesser extent by domestic companies (well-known examples include AT&T's Bell Labs and IBM's research labs) into the product of multinational teams of researchers working in international clusters (e.g., Silicon Valley or Bangalore) of emerging tech firms, capital markets, and research universities (Segal, 2004), with an increasing role of private sector funding. Thus, companies increasingly see investment in innovation as a profitable use of funds that can help in locating new resources (e.g., oil, gas, or mineral deposits), creating new products (e.g., pharmaceuticals, information technology devices), improving their productive processes (e.g., computer-aided design, workflow analyses, shipment planning, medical diagnosis), and decreasing the cost of production (e.g., capital/labor substitution; paperless offices; improved crop planning, fertilization, irrigation, and harvesting).

Many advanced nations are expanding investments in S&T to develop their economies. The U.S., Europe (EU-15),[2] and Japan today account for about 74 percent of world R&D expenditures, down from 84 percent in 1993. U.S. R&D expenditures grew at an average rate of 5.8 percent per year, close to the world's average of 6.4 percent, allowing the U.S. share of world expenditures to remain fairly stable over the period 1993-2006. The U.S. share was 35.6 percent in 2006, down from 38.7 percent in 1993. During this period, the EU-15 share decreased from 29.2 percent to 23.9 percent and that of Japan fell from 16.3 percent to 14.4 percent. R&D spending increased rapidly in South Korea, China, Russia, and the rest of the world, growing at 10.4, 18.3, 7.0, and 8.0 percent on average per year, respectively. China's R&D expenditures grew fastest, driving the nation's share from 2.3 percent to 9.0 percent.

R&D intensity is measured as the ratio of gross domestic expenditure on R&D (GERD) to gross domestic product (GDP). For the period 1985 to 2006 it was relatively high for the U.S. at 2.6 percent and fairly stable over time. In the EU-15 it remained constant at 1.8 percent over the period. Only Japan has had a consistently higher R&D intensity than the U.S.,[3] and it increased from 2.4 percent in 1985 to 3.4 percent in 2006. The R&D intensities of Korea and China have also increased, with Korea's growing from 1.8 percent to 3.2 percent and China's growing from 0.7 percent to 1.4 percent between 1991 and 2006. The rapid increases in Korea and especially China are consistent with the decline in the share of world R&D spending from the U.S., EU-15, and Japan.[4] Overall, the change in shares among countries comes from the relatively greater increase in R&D spending in other countries, especially China and Korea, which began from a relatively low base, rather than a decrease in R&D spending in the U.S., Europe, or Japan. Hence, we emphasize the R&D rise of other nations.

The U.S. employs more S&T researchers than any other geographic region, with 1.39 million full-time equivalent researchers (FTE; OECD Science, Technology and Industry Outlook, 2008). But the EU-15 with 1.13 million, China with 1.12 million and Japan with 0.70 million (all FTE) also have sizeable S&T workforces. U.S. growth in S&T employment averaged 3.0 percent per year from 1995 to 2005, slightly below the industrialized nations of the OECD and EU-15 averages of 3.3 percent, and above that of Japan, 2.5 percent. According to OECD estimates, China surpassed Japan and now matches the EU-15 in S&T employment as a result of rapid growth of 7.9 percent per year over the period 1995 to 2005. China added a large number of researchers, 597,000, between 1995 and 2005, while the U.S. added 352,000, the EU-15 added 308,000, and Japan added 153,000.[5]

As China has emerged as a major economic power, it has greatly increased the number of scientists and engineers produced by its universities. In 2004 the EU-15 and China graduated more scientists and engineers than did the U.S., Japan, or Russia (Figure 7.1). The EU-15 and China had about 617,000 and 672,000 new graduates, respectively, versus 456,000 for the U.S., 349,000 (2005) for Japan and 294,000 (2006) for Russia.[6]

FIGURE 7.1: FIRST UNIVERSITY DEGREES IN S&E (2004)

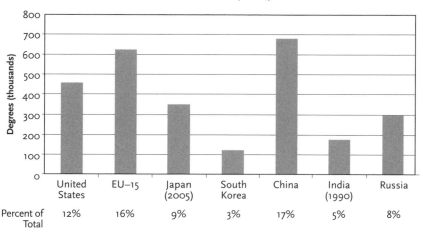

Source: National Science Board (2008).

These various indicators of input to a nation's S&E enterprise—R&D spending, R&D intensity, researchers and new S&E graduates—show the significant advancement of developing nations such as China and South Korea. At the same time, developed nations such as the U.S., Europe and Japan show no clear signs of slowing down relative to their trend. U.S. total R&D, basic research, and federally funded basic research expenditures as well as spending by universities and colleges have grown significantly at 4 to 6 percent in real terms (except for total R&D, which grew by 3.4 percent per year on average in the last decade) and in line with historic growth rates. The relatively stable R&D intensity in the U.S. and Europe suggests that their R&D expenditures grew roughly in line with their economies. Japan's R&D expenditures grew faster than its economy, indicating Japan's ongoing commitment to R&D even during the 1990s when its economy grew slowly.

As developing nations increase the share of their GDP spent on R&D and developed nations sustain their share, R&D becomes a larger part of the global economy. Will this ultimately translate into accelerated discovery and innovation worldwide and are we perhaps seeing the beginnings of this? Let's turn our attention to publications, citations and patents—indicators of research and innovation output.

Global Acceleration of Discovery and Invention?

Figure 7.2 shows the world shares of research publications (upper panel) and top 1 percent most cited publications (lower panel) for the period 1995 to 2005. Publications are a measure of research output and top 1 percent most cited publications are a measure of the impact and quality of research output.[7]

Given populations of roughly 0.3 billion (U.S.), 0.5 billion (EU-27), and over 2.5 billion (Asia-10), the research output of the U.S. on a per capita basis is extraordinary. But as the panels in Figure 2 show, other regions are advancing in output, especially Asia, and in impact, which has the effect of reducing the U.S. share.

FIGURE 7.2:
SHARE OF WORLD S&T PUBLICATIONS BY NATION/REGION (1995-2005)

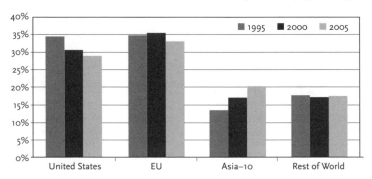

SHARE OF WORLD'S TOP 1 PERCENT MOST CITED S&T PUBLICATIONS BY NATION/REGION (1995-2005)

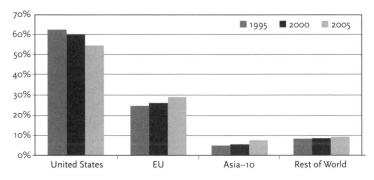

Source: National Science Board (2008).

Patents are one of the most commonly used indicators of innovative activity. Figure 7.3 shows world triadic patents by region from 1985 to 2005. Triadic patent families are a set of inventions that are patented broadly in the U.S., Europe and Japan. To improve the timeliness of triadic patent data, the OECD presents estimated counts for recent years (Dernis, 2007).[8] As seen, the U.S., Europe and Japan dominate patenting, accounting for more than 90 percent of world triadic patents, and their individual shares are now about the same at roughly 30 percent. Japan's growth rate in triadic patents has been faster than that of the EU-15 and the U.S. Korea is starting to become a significant player, but China and Russia, despite significant inputs (see previous section) and rapid growth rates, still have a minimal footprint. Eaton and Kortum (2007) suggest that China's rapid growth has resulted from absorbing foreign technology rather than from domestic innovation.

FIGURE 7.3: TRIADIC PATENTS AS PERCENTAGE OF TOTAL WORLD PATENTS (1985-2005)

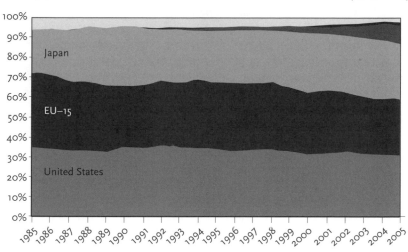

Source: www.oecd.org/sti/ipr-statistics.

These patterns suggest that while global S&T outputs are still largely produced by developed nations, we may be facing a future of global acceleration of innovation and discovery as developing nations such as China and India could follow in the footsteps of Japan and Korea and become innovators as they continue to develop their S&E enterprises.

Implications of the Globalization of S&T and the Rise of Other Nations in S&T

The most common concern expressed by experts in developed nations such as the U.S., Europe and Japan regarding the rise of other nations is that it signals the decline of developed nations' competitiveness in S&T. But neither globalization nor S&T progress is a zero-sum game, and improvement in one country does not necessarily imply a loss for another country. In fact, the globalization of S&T and the rise of other nations in S&T can be beneficial to developed nations as well as to developing nations. But there are uncertainties, and developed nations cannot assume these trends will necessarily benefit them.

First, the globalization of S&T can be seen as a continuation of the general trend (now increasingly in the realm of technology) towards increased global interconnectivity and trade. The globalization of trade and commerce, propelled by lower costs of shipping and communication and lower trade barriers, creates gains from trade and aids the economic development of trading partners. This benefits developed nations via specialization, cheaper imports, and larger export markets, and developing nations through their economic development. Over the last several decades as globalization gained new dimensions, the U.S. and Europe experienced fairly steady economic growth and significant job creation. This is not to obscure the fact that increased trade can disrupt domestic industries, displace workers from their jobs, and affect wages. The article by Krugman (2008) and comment by Lawrence (2008), for instance, discuss how trade can affect wages, with Krugman arguing that increased trade has reduced the relative wage of low-skilled U.S. workers and thereby created greater income inequality, and Lawrence arguing that "there is no longer evidence of growing wage inequality that supports a simple story of pervasive and growing differences in the rewards to skill" (p. 150).

Second, developed nations may benefit from new technology invented elsewhere. As Eaton and Kortum (2007) discuss, the pool of new technology, not yet acquired and not yet implemented at home, is much larger for developing nations than it is for already developed nations, allowing developing nations to increase productivity by absorbing the technology and hence to grow much more rapidly. Developed nations must rely mostly on recent innovations made at home or abroad (a much smaller pool of new technology) to increase productivity, and thus are growing more slowly. They typically must also bear the cost of those innovations. But, the rise of developing nations' capacity in S&T suggests that the global pool of technology will grow more rapidly than in the past as both developed and developing nations contribute to it. As we have seen, loss of world share in some measures of S&T inputs and outputs by developed nations does not appear to be the result of a slackening in their S&T effort but signals "catching up" by developing nations. The increasingly widespread diffusion of knowledge as a result of the globalization of S&T in turn suggests that more countries can participate in applying that knowledge to the production of goods and services, which has the potential of increasing economic growth, incomes, and living standards in many lands.

Third, it is not obvious that the globalization of S&T will work to the detriment of the S&E enterprise in advanced nations. The demand for research may increase in nations that are better at it (currently, broadly the U.S., Europe and Japan). Eaton and Kortum (2006) explore innovation activity of nations using a two-country (North and South) Ricardian model of innovation, technology diffusion, and trade, with each country having two sectors, one producing R&D and the other producing a tradable good. The model suggests some surprising implications of the greater diffusion of ideas and lower trade barriers associated with globalization: as long as trade barriers are not too high, faster diffusion of innovations shifts research activity toward the country better at creating them. This shift increases the relative wage in the S&T sector there. It can even mean that, with more diffusion, the country better at research attains a larger share of technologies in its exclusive domain.

But ultimately, if current trends are continued, centers of excellence on par with those in developed nations will arise in developing nations. These emergent centers could cause a shift in comparative advantage from developed to developing nations. Of particular concern to developed nations are populous low-income countries such as China and India that can compete in high tech by having many S&T workers and a low wage advantage (Freeman, 2006, 2007). Loss of comparative advantage in a high-tech sector to a low wage competitor can substantially harm an advanced country, as it must shift resources to other sectors and more of the profits from new products or innovations shift from the developed to the less developed country.

The Migration of S&T Talent

Growth in S&E degrees (bachelor's degree or higher) has been 1-2 percent per year for the past three decades in the U.S. Despite public opinion to the contrary, the growth in S&E degrees has been similar to, not lower than, the growth rates in other fields (e.g., Galama & Hosek, 2007b). But an increasing share of S&E degrees is being awarded to foreign students, particularly at the master's and doctoral level, and this is especially true in the field of engineering (Figure 7.4). The share of doctorate degrees in engineering awarded to foreigners was nearly 60 percent in 2005. The foreign share of doctorate degrees went up from 21 to 36 percent (average over all fields) between 1985 and 2005 and the share of master's degrees from 19 to 28 percent while it remained stable at 4 percent for bachelor's and 2 to 3 percent for associate's degrees.

Have apparently slow degree growth and the fact that a smaller and smaller share of S&E degrees are awarded to U.S. citizens led to shortages of S&E workers in the U.S.? An analysis of Current Population Survey (CPS) data of the S&E workforce[9] does not suggest shortages of workers over the period 1993 to 2005 (Galama & Hosek, 2007b). Traditional indicators of shortage are low unemployment and/or high wage growth relative to past trends and compared to other high skill occupations. But the unemployment rate of S&E workers is similar to that of non-S&E workers[10] with similar levels of education and there are no signs of unusual wage growth. Real wages grew by 0.9 percent per year for scientists and engineers, compared with 0.8 percent for lawyers, 1.8 percent for medical doctors and 0.3 percent for other occupations.

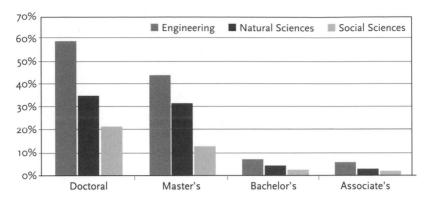

Source: National Science Board (2008).
Note: Temporary residents only (permanent residents are not included). Share of foreign doctoral students may be higher as a significant fraction of the sample is reported with unknown status (this is not the case for master's, bachelor's and associate's degrees). An upper limit can be obtained by assuming that all individuals with unknown status are temporary residents. In that case, the share of foreign recipients of doctoral degrees in engineering, natural sciences and social sciences is, respectively, 64, 40 and 27 percent.

Perhaps surprisingly, S&E employment has significantly outpaced degree production in all S&E fields over the period 1980 to 2000 (Figure 7.5). This trend appears to continue well into 2005 with occupational employment in S&E growing by 4.5 percent per year (CPS) and degree production by 3.4 percent per year (National Science Board, 2008) from 2000 to 2005. The S&E workforce thus grew at an average rate of more than 4.2 percent per year between 1980 and 2005, filling a total of 2.7 million jobs and more than doubling the S&E workforce (4.2 million workers in 2005 according to CPS data) over the period.

This leads one to wonder where these workers are coming from. Apart from the traditional path—a U.S. citizen graduating with a degree in S&E and joining the S&E workforce—there are two alternative paths. First, many U.S. citizens are entering S&E careers from other occupations. These individuals may have been educated in S&E and at some point entered a non-S&E field; the total pool of individuals with S&E degrees is estimated to be between 14.5 and 21.4 million[11] workers, much larger than the actual number of S&E workers, estimated to be between 3.9 and 5.0 million[12] (National Science Board, 2008). In addition, some S&E workers do not hold S&E degrees, suggesting the total pool of potential S&E workers is even larger.

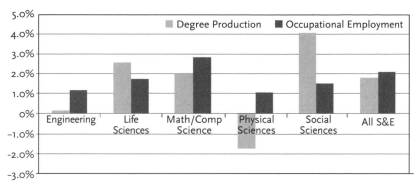

Source: National Science Board (2006).

Second, a growing number of S&E workers are immigrants. The share of foreigners in the S&E workforce increased from 6 percent in 1994 to 12 percent in 2006, while the share of foreigners in the non-S&E workforce remained constant at about 5 percent over the period. Many foreign S&E workers enter the U.S. labor force directly with advanced degrees obtained abroad or they enter through the education route, obtaining an advanced degree in the U.S. and subsequently deciding to stay. Evidence suggests that foreign S&E talent increasingly decided to stay in the U.S. and stay for long periods of time, even indefinitely.[13] This is contrary to the perceptions that a large fraction of talented foreign S&E graduates return home, or that the fraction returning home has been increasing as other regions of the world develop S&T capacity and provide attractive opportunities. Still, the development of foreign science centers may cause more foreign scientists and engineers to return home in future years or to develop an affiliation with centers in their home country.

Foreign scientists and engineers in the U.S. are young. The increase in the percentage of non-U.S. citizens in S&E has been the greatest among younger S&E workers. Non-U.S. citizens now number one in five among S&E workers ages 21-35, and this is about twice the overall percentage across all worker ages. And, they are talented. That is, foreign S&E workers have similar average earnings and similar earnings distributions (Figure 7.6) as U.S. citizen S&E workers, suggesting that they are of equal quality and skill, and as productive as U.S. citizens. This is not the case for the non-S&E workforce, where foreigners are paid about 15 percent less on average.

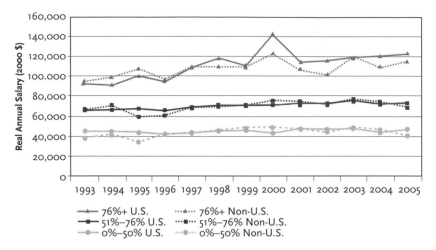

Source: RAND analysis of Current Population Survey data. For details see Galama and Hosek, 2007b. Percentages refer to income distribution; for example, the 76%+ lines track the average income for the highest-paid one-fourth of workers over time.

High-skilled Immigrants are Crucial to Competitiveness in S&T

Some are concerned that the U.S. is becoming vulnerable as a result of its increasing reliance on foreign S&E workers. Essential positions are being filled by foreigners who eventually may return home, taking valuable and in some cases critical skills with them. But the U.S. continues to be a net recipient of foreign S&E talent—the share of foreigners has increased, not decreased—and foreigners have been increasingly likely to stay. Contrast this with most other regions of the world that are exporters of foreign S&E talent and worried about losing their best and brightest to this "brain drain."

Foreign S&E workers in the U.S. do not appear to be taking jobs from U.S. citizens. The share of foreigners in the S&E workforce is still small, at 12 percent, and most of the rapid growth in S&E jobs went to U.S. citizens. U.S. citizen S&E workers have low unemployment, and their wages have grown faster than for non-S&E workers (but slower than in medicine and law). There appears to be ample room for both U.S. citizens and foreigners in S&E.

Further, foreign S&E workers play an important role in ensuring that U.S. firms are competitive and continue to invest in the U.S. Access to S&E talent is crucial for innovation and efficiency, and if firms cannot fill their S&E positions domestically, then offshoring their R&D operations becomes an attractive option. A study based on the 2006 Duke/Booz Allen Hamilton Offshoring Research Network Survey (Couto et al., 2006) suggests that offshoring was a tactical labor cost-saving exercise but is now increasingly driven by the need to access scarce talent. Further, the study finds that the more sophisticated or high-skilled the function, the lower is the impact of offshoring on employment in the originating country. In contrast, offshoring routine back-office functions does result in lost jobs. This is in line with economic research finding that skilled labor and capital are complements, whereas unskilled labor and capital are substitutes (e.g., Autor, et al, 2006).

Under H1-B visas, skilled foreigners may be employed temporarily in specialty occupations. The sharp reduction in the annual H1-B visa cap from a peak of 195,000 in the years 2001 to 2003, to 65,000 in the years thereafter may increase offshoring and outsourcing and reduce investment at home (i.e., loss of future jobs for Americans). It may not even induce greater numbers of U.S. citizens to join the S&E workforce, as wage growth will still be slowed by the decision to offshore or outsource the work. Increasing the inflow of foreign high-skill S&E workers may, in contrast, increase investment and employment at home as well as provide local spillover benefits.

Global Competition for Skilled Workers is Likely to Intensify

As mentioned, many countries are increasingly vying to build their S&T capacity, and this is likely to lead to an increasing global demand for scientists, engineers, and other skilled workers. The EU is concerned that it is becoming more difficult to meet Europe's growing demand for high-skilled labor as the demographic gap widens and students shy away from scientific and technical studies (Euractiv, 2008). The EU has not been as successful as the U.S., Canada, Australia or New Zealand in its effort to attract S&E talent from developing nations such as China and India. To counter this trend, the EU is in the process of introducing a "blue" card, a proposed work permit allowing high-skilled non-EU citizens to work and live in any country within the EU. The aim of the blue card is to compete with the U.S. green card and attract up to 20 million highly skilled workers from outside the EU (Euractiv, 2008).

Trends in the U.S. and abroad suggest that global competition for college-educated workers will intensify in the future as a result of demographic trends. Between 1980 and 2000 the U.S. added 20 million workers with college degrees to the labor force, which more than doubled the college-educated workforce. But in stark contrast, between 2000 and 2020 only 8 million additions to this workforce are anticipated, as baby boomers are beginning to retire and fewer prime-age workers will join the labor force (Ellwood, 2001).

Many nations in addition to the U.S. face an aging population, and in fact other nations appear to be worse off in this respect. The college-age population decreased in Europe, the U.S., China, and Japan in the 1990s and is projected to continue to decrease in Europe, Japan, and China, while that of the U.S. will grow modestly. By 2025 the population ages 18-23 (a proxy for the college-age population) of the U.S. is forecast to be 5 percent larger than in 2005 (National Science Board, 2006). Western Europe, China, and Japan will see decreases of 8 percent, 14 percent, and 16 percent, respectively. These decreases in the college-age population, the National Science

Board report (2006) notes, may be an incentive for countries to encourage immigration of students from other countries or to increase enrollment proportions of their own college-age population.

Summary and Conclusions

The nature of innovation has changed from a largely publicly funded to a largely privately funded endeavor and has become much more global. As developed nations continue to invest in R&D and as developing nations are catching up with developed nations, various S&T inputs (e.g., R&D spending, researchers and new S&E graduates) show strong global growth. While this is not immediately translating into significant S&T outputs (e.g., patents, but with the exception perhaps of research publications and citations), ultimately as developing nations build S&T capabilities global innovation and discovery are expected to accelerate. China, for example, already appears to have a research workforce comparable in size to that of Europe, larger than Japan's and only slightly smaller than that of the U.S. China also accounts for nearly 10 percent of global expenditures on R&D. But China does not appear to be a major innovator yet as reflected in its relatively small footprint in global patents. South Korea began its development trajectory earlier than China and appears to be starting to make an impact. China and other developing nations may very well follow in Korea's footsteps.

The U.S. is a net recipient of foreign S&E talent while most other nations are senders. Foreigners have helped enable fast growth of the U.S. S&E workforce in the face of slow growth in degree production. Foreign S&E talent appears to be of equal quality and skill and as productive as U.S. native-born S&E. Rather than taking jobs from Americans, foreign scientists and engineers could be essential to ensuring that U.S. firms remain competitive and that investment in R&D takes place in the U.S. rather than overseas. Significant global investment in S&T and demographic changes are likely to increase the demand for scientists and engineers worldwide. For example, Europe is seeking to emulate the U.S. by attracting 20 million high-skilled workers from non-EU countries through immigration reform focused on the highly skilled.

While the rise of the developing world in S&T appears worrisome to many in the developed world, there are many reasons to suggest that it should be welcomed. Not only is it good for developing nations to build S&T capability, educate their populations and create high-paying jobs, but developed nations can benefit from larger, more global S&T as well. Scientific and technological development is not a zero-sum game. For one, the pie is getting bigger, with global R&D and global employment in S&E growing rapidly. And, inventions made elsewhere can benefit nations that are able to make use of them; developed nations are particularly well positioned in this regard. But there are uncertainties, including the likelihood that developing nations will gain comparative advantage in certain areas of S&T. And there is the possibility that the competition for S&E talent will intensify. This may be of particular concern to the

Unites States, to date a major beneficiary of global immigration flows of the highly skilled. Developed nations may be well advised to establish connections with up-and-coming centers of excellence to learn from and be part of their scientific discoveries.

NOTES

[1] Nearly 80 percent of journal literature in science was published in the English language in the 2000s, up from about 60 percent in the 1980s.

[2] The EU-15 consists of Austria, Belgium, Denmark, Finland, France, Germany, Greece, Ireland, Italy, Luxembourg, the Netherlands, Portugal, Spain, Sweden, and the United Kingdom.

[3] A number of EU-15 countries also have higher R&D intensities. The comparison is made between regions of similar size, i.e. the EU-15, U.S., Japan, China, etc. In addition, data are not always available for individual nations (e.g., India).

[4] The R&D intensity of the Russian Federation grew quickly from 0.7 percent in 1992 (a low point that followed a steep drop from 2.0 percent in 1990) to 1.1 percent in 2006. But due to its smaller economy and relatively lower economic growth compared with China (even though growth was much faster than in the U.S., EU-15 and Japan), total R&D growth is much smaller and contributes relatively little to the decline in world share of the U.S., EU-15 and Japan.

[5] The OECD notes that many of the 2005 figures (and even many of the earlier data points) are estimates or projections rather than validated counts. This can result in abrupt changes when projections are updated. It should therefore be noted that the significant growth in the number of China FTE researchers is the result of one year: between 2004 and 2005 China added 193,000 researchers according to the OECD, representing nearly a third of the total researchers added between 1995 and 2005.

[6] Estimates of the number of graduates are hindered by differences in science and engineering classification as well as by international differences in degrees (e.g., the Anglo-Saxon bachelor's degree versus the German *Diplom*), in the quality of education, and in the duration of programs. As a result, various sources report different numbers. Nevertheless the various sources consistently find that the European Union and China graduate more scientists and engineers than the United States does (see Galama and Hosek, 2007 for a more detailed discussion).

[7] Unfortunately, data are not available for the same nations or regions as in other figures. The EU in Figure 7.2 is the EU-27, and Asia-10 consists of China, India, Indonesia, Japan, Malaysia, Philippines, Singapore, South Korea, Taiwan, and Thailand.

[8] Patent data face issues of timeliness as there are a) legal delays before a patent's content is publicly released and b) a backlog of patent filings that have not been processed or published at the U.S. patent office (Dernis, 2007). Owing to time lag between the priority date and the availability of information (especially for U.S. Patent Trade Office grants), 1999 is the latest year for which triadic patent families are almost completely available (page 8 of the OECD's 2008 Compendium of Patent Statistics). Therefore, data for the latest years are OECD estimates based on more recent series (Dernis, 2007).

Patent data were revised substantially between 2006 and 2008 by the OECD for recent years (compare the 2008 Compendium of Patent Statistics with earlier compendia). Compared to Galama and Hosek (2007b; Figure 2.6), the revised estimates in Figure 7.3 show a slightly different picture: while U.S. patenting still grows faster than in Europe, recent data suggest it grew slower than in Japan. In addition, the rapid growth of Korea was less apparent in earlier data.

[9] Defined as individuals with a bachelor's degree or higher (in any field) who work in science and engineering.

[10] Exceptions occurred in the 1991 recession and the dot-com bust in the late 1990s, and in both cases the S&E

workforce had a higher unemployment rate than the non-S&E workforce. This would be evidence of an excess of S&E workers rather than a shortage.

[11] These estimates are based on NSF SESTAT data for 2006. The 14.5 million concerns individuals with a bachelor's degree or more and with their highest degree in an S&E field. The 21.4 million estimate concerns individuals with a bachelor's degree or higher and any degree in S&E or an S&E related field.

[12] Based on 2005 American Community Survey data (3.9 million) and 2006 NSF SESTAT data (5.0 million).

[13] The two-year stay rate (rate at which an individual is found to be in the U.S. two years after graduation) of foreign recipients of doctorate degrees in S&E from U.S. universities has increased from 50 percent in 1989 to 67 percent in 2005 (Finn, 2007). In addition, long-term (five- and ten-year) stay rates track short-term stay rates closely, suggesting that long-term stay rates are currently near 67 percent as well. Similar information is not available for foreigners with other degrees (master's, bachelor's) or foreigners who obtained their education abroad.

REFERENCES

Autor, D. H., Katz, L. F., & Kearney, M. S. (2006). *The polarization of the U.S. labor market.* Cambridge, MA: National Bureau of Economic Research. Working Paper 11986. Retrieved February 28, 2008, from www.nber.org/papers/w11986.pdf

Couto, V., Mani, M., Lewin, A. Y. & Peeters, C. (2006). *The globalization of white-collar work: The facts and fallout of next-generation offshoring.* McLean, VA: Booz Allen Hamilton. Retrieved February 28, 2008, from www.boozallen.com/media/file/Globalization_White_Collar_Work_v3.pdf

Dernis, H. (2007). *Nowcasting patent indicators.* STI Working Paper 2007/3 Statistical Analysis of Science, Technology and Industry, JT03233402. Retrieved February 19, 2009, from www.oecd.org/dataoecd/0/20/39485567.pdf

Eaton, J., & Kortum, S. (2006, July). *Innovation, diffusion, and trade.* Cambridge, MA: National Bureau of Economic Research, Working Paper 12385. Retrieved January 8, 2009, from www.nber.org/papers/w12385

Eaton, J., & Kortum, S. (2007). National security in a knowledge based global economy. In Galama, T. J. & Hosek, J. (Eds.), *Perspectives on U.S. competitiveness in science and technology.* Santa Monica, CA: RAND Corporation. CF-325-OSD. Retrieved January 8, 2009, from www.rand.org/pubs/conf_proceedings/CF235

Ellwood, D. T. (2001). The sputtering labor force of the twenty-first century: Can the U.S. experience be sustained and replicated? In Krueger, A., & Solow, R. (Eds.), *The roaring nineties: Can full employment be sustained?* (pp.421-489). New York: Russell Sage Foundation.

Euractiv. (2008, April 22). An EU 'Blue Card' for high-skilled immigrants? Retrieved January 8, 2009, from www.euractiv.com/en/socialeurope/eu-blue-card-high-skilled-immigrants/article-170986

Euractiv. (2004, August 17) Lisbon Agenda. Retrieved December 28, 2008, from www.euractiv.com/en/future-eu/lisbon-agenda/article-117510

Finn, M. G. (2007). *Stay rates of foreign doctorate recipients from U.S. universities, 2005.* Oak Ridge, TN: Oak Ridge Institute for Science and Education. Retrieved January 6, 2009, from http://orise.orau.gov/sep/files/stayrate07.pdf

Freeman, R. (2006). *Does globalization of the scientific engineering workforce threaten U.S. economic leadership?* Cambridge, MA: National Bureau of Economic Research. Working Paper 11457. Retrieved January 8, 2009, from www.nber.org/papers/w11457

Freeman, R. (2007). Globalization of the scientific/engineering workforce and national security. In Galama, T. J. & Hosek, J. (Eds.), *Perspectives on U.S. competitiveness in science and technology.* Santa Monica, CA: RAND Corporation. CF-325-OSD. Retrieved January 8, 2009, from www.rand.org/pubs/conf_proceedings/CF235

Galama, T. J., & Hosek, J. (Eds.). (2007a). *Perspectives on U.S. competitiveness in science and technology*. Santa Monica, CA: RAND Corporation. CF-325-OSD. Retrieved December 28, 2008, from www.rand.org/pubs/conf_proceedings/CF235

Galama, T. J., & Hosek, J. (Eds.). (2007b). *U.S. competitiveness in science and technology*. Santa Monica, CA: RAND Corporation. MG-674-OSD. Retrieved December 28, 2008, from www.rand.org/pubs/monographs/MG674

Krugman, P. (2008). Trade and wages, reconsidered. *Brookings papers on economic activity, Spring 2008*, 103-137.

Lawrence, R. Z. (2008). Comment on 'trade and wages, reconsidered.' *Brookings papers on economic activity, Spring 2008*, 149-153.

Montgomery, S. (2004). Of towers, walls, and fields: Perspectives on language in science. *Science, 303:5662*, 1333-1335.

National Science Board. (2006). *Science and engineering indicators 2006*. Retrieved December 28, 2008, from www.nsf.gov/statistics/seind06

National Science Board. (2008). *Science and engineering indicators 2008*. Retrieved December 28, 2008, from www.nsf.gov/statistics/seind08

Organisation for Economic Co-operation and Development (2008). *OECD science, technology and industry outlook, 2008*. Retrieved December 28, 2008, from www.oecd.org/document/36/0,3343,en_2649_34273_41546660_1_1_1_1,00.html

Organisation for Economic Co-operation and Development (2008). *2008 compendium of patent statistics*. Retrieved December 28, 2008, from www.sciencearchived.com/oecd-compendium-of-patent-statistics-2008

Segal, A. (2004). Is America losing its edge? Innovation in a globalized world. *Foreign Affairs, 83:6*, 2-8. Retrieved December 28, 2008, from www.foreignaffairs.org/20041101facomment83601/adam-segal/is-america-losing-its-edge.html

Chapter Eight

NEW DEVELOPMENTS AND UNINTENDED CONSEQUENCES: WHITHER THOU GOEST, INTERNATIONALIZATION?

BY JANE KNIGHT, UNIVERSITY OF TORONTO

As we progress into the 21ˢᵗ century, the international dimension of higher education is becoming increasingly important, and at the same time, much more complex. The changing dynamics of internationalization are contributing to the current state of turmoil in the higher education sector (Knight, 2008a). During the last decade, there have been new actors, new rationales, new programs, new regulations, and new developments in globalization. Internationalization has become a formidable force for change, as many developments and initiatives in higher education demonstrate.

As internationalization adapts to meet new challenges, it is important to examine the key concepts that inform and shape the internationalization process and sometimes result in unexpected developments and unanticipated results. The following discussion acknowledges the multiple and varied benefits attributed to internationalization, but the primary focus is on the unintended consequences that need to be addressed and monitored.

The Confusion and Complexity of "Internationalization"

Internationalization is a term that means different things to different people. While it is encouraging to see the increased use and attention being given to the term, there is a great deal of confusion about what internationalization means.

For some people, it means a series of international activities such as academic mobility for students and teachers; international networks, partnerships and projects; and new international academic programs and research initiatives. For others it means delivering education to other countries through new types of arrangements such as branch campuses or franchises using a variety of face-to-face and distance techniques. To many, it means including an international, intercultural and/or global dimension into the curriculum and teaching-learning process. Still others see internationalization as a means to improve national or world rankings of their institution or to recruit the best and brightest international students and scholars. International development projects have traditionally been perceived as part of internationalization, and more

Recent Developments and Initiatives in Higher Education

- Development of new international networks and consortia
- The growing numbers of students, professors, and researchers participating in academic mobility schemes
- Increases in the number of courses, programs, and qualifications that focus on comparative and international themes
- More emphasis placed on developing international/intercultural and global competencies
- Stronger interest in international themes and collaborative research
- A growing number of academic programs delivered across borders
- More interest and concern with international and regional rankings of universities
- An increase in campus-based extracurricular activities with an international or multicultural component
- Increased attention given to recruiting foreign students
- Rising numbers of joint and double degree programs
- Growth in the number and types of for-profit cross-border education providers
- Expansion of partnerships, franchises and branch campuses
- Creation of regional education hubs, education cities and gateways
- Establishment of new national, regional, and international organizations focused on international education

recently the increasing emphasis on trade in higher education has also been seen as internationalization. Finally, there is frequent confusion about the relationship of internationalization with globalization. Is internationalization the same as globalization, as far as higher education is concerned? If so, why, how and to what end? If not, how is it different or what is the relationship between these two dynamic processes?

In addition to questions about definition, other important issues are being raised about internationalization, questions such as: What is the purpose of internationalization? What are the expected benefits or outcomes? What are the values that underpin it? What are the positive consequences, unintended results and negative implications? What about new risks attached to internationalization? How are institutions and policymakers responding to the competing interests within the domain of internationalization? What are the funding implications? How are governments and NGOs addressing the issue and moving forward? Are for-profit and non-profit internationalization strategies compatible? Does internationalization have a role in brain drain, homogenization/hybridization of culture, or international labor mobility? As the internationalization agenda changes, these are clearly important issues and questions that require close scrutiny.

Defining Internationalization

"Internationalization" as a term is not new, nor is the debate over its meaning. Internationalization has been used for years in political science and government, but its popularity in the education sector has really soared only since the early 1980s. Prior to this time, "international education" and "international cooperation" were favored terms and still are in some countries. In the 1990s, discussions on terminology centered on differentiating "international education" from such overlapping terms as "comparative education," "global education," and "multicultural education." But today, the relationships and nuances of meaning among "cross-border," "transnational," "borderless," and "international" modes of education are more important and cause much confusion.

The challenging part of developing a definition for "internationalization" is the need for it to be generic enough to apply to many different countries, cultures and education systems. This is no easy task. While it is not necessarily the intention to develop a universal definition, it is imperative that it can be used in a broad range of contexts and for comparative purposes across countries and regions of the world. With this in mind, it is important to ensure that a definition does not specify the rationales, benefits, outcomes, actors, activities, and stakeholders of internationalization, as they vary enormously across nations and also from institution to institution. What is critical is that the international dimension relates to all aspects of education and the role that it plays in society. In previous publications, I have defined internationalization as "the process of integrating an international, intercultural or global dimension into the purpose, functions or delivery of higher education" (Knight, 2004, p.9).

This definition of internationalization is intentionally neutral. Many would argue that the process of internationalization should be described in terms of promoting cooperation and solidarity among nations, improving quality and relevance of higher education, or contributing to the advancement of research for international issues. While these are noble intentions and internationalization can contribute to these goals, a definition needs to be objective enough that it can be used to describe a phenomenon that is in fact, universal, but which has different purposes and outcomes, depending on the actor or stakeholder.

A significant development in the conceptualization of internationalization in the last five years has been the introduction of the terms "internationalization at home" and "cross-border education." Campus-based strategies are most often referred to as internationalization "at home" and off-campus initiatives are called "cross-border education." As a result of a heightened emphasis on international academic mobility, institutions have developed the "at home" concept to give greater prominence to campus-based elements such as the intercultural and international dimension in the teaching-learning process, research, extra-curricular activities, relationships with local cultural and ethnic community groups, as well as the integration of foreign students and scholars into campus life and activities. The internationalization process consists of these two separate but closely linked and interdependent pillars (Knight, 2008a).

Cross-border education has significant implications for campus-based internationalization and vice versa.

New Developments and Unintended Consequences

The Brain Train

Twenty-five years ago, we could not have anticipated that international academic mobility for students, scholars and professors would have the potential to grow into a highly competitive international recruitment business. Today, several countries such as Australia, Germany and the UK are investing in major marketing campaigns to attract the best and brightest talent to study and work in their institutions in order to meet the heavy demand from government and private industry for human resources for innovation and research agendas (Agarwal et al., 2007). The original goal of helping students from developing countries move to another country to complete a degree and return home is fading fast as nations compete for retaining brain power.

While "brain drain" and "brain gain" are well-known concepts, research is showing a more complex picture. International students and researchers are increasingly interested in earning multiple degrees in multiple countries, before perhaps returning to their home countries after eight to twelve years of international study and work experience. Hence, the emergence of the term "brain train." These various "brain circulation" concepts present benefits, risks and new challenges for both sending and receiving countries. Higher education is becoming a more important actor in policy-making and is now working in closer collaboration with immigration, industry and the science and technology sectors to build an integrated strategy for attracting and retaining knowledge workers.

Is the Quality of New Cross-Border Education Being Assured?

The Singapore Ministry of Trade and Industry estimates that the higher education sector is a $2.2 trillion market (Ministry of Trade and Industry, 2003). Furthermore, it is forecasted that by 2025 the demand for international education will grow to 7.2 million students—a quantum leap from 1.2 million students in 2000 (Bohm et al., 2002). These staggering figures—which represent global demand for all forms of internationalization, including student mobility and cross-border program delivery through franchising, twinning, double and joint degrees, and branch campuses, etc.—illustrate the magnitude of the interest in international education. Some, but certainly not all of this demand, will be met by student mobility. Consequently, the number of new providers, such as commercial companies and non-governmental entities, that deliver programs to students in their home countries is accelerating at an unprecedented rate. It is no longer just students, faculty, researchers who are internationally mobile—academic degree/diploma programs are being delivered across borders, and branch campuses are being established in developing and developed countries around the world. While these new developments are intended to increase access to higher education and meet the appetite for foreign credentials, there are serious issues related to the quality of the academic offerings, the integrity of the new types of providers, and the recognition of credentials (Vincent-Lancrin, 2004).

In the last decade, increased importance has been given to quality assurance at the institutional and national levels. New regional quality networks have also been established. The primary task of these groups has been quality recognition and assurance of domestic higher education provision by public and private higher education institutions. However, the increase in cross-border education by institutions and new private commercial providers has introduced a new challenge (and gap) in the field of quality assurance. Historically, national quality assurance agencies have generally not focused their efforts on assessing the quality of imported and exported programs. The question now facing the field of quality assurance is how to deal with the increase in cross-border education, delivered both by traditional higher education institutions and also by new private commercial providers who have not historically been included in nationally based quality assurance projects (Knight, 2007).

It is probable that the task of developing international quality standards and procedures for cross-border education will not be limited to the higher education sector alone. ISO standards (industry-based mechanisms to ensure the quality of manufactured products and services) are examples of quality assessment systems that might be adapted to cross-border education. Professionals in the education sector have mixed views on the appropriateness of quality standards being established by those outside the sector. In fact, opinions differ on the value of implementing any international quality assurance standards or criteria, as imposing such standards might jeopardize the sovereignty of national-level systems and do little to improve the actual quality of these programs.

The Internationalization and Commercialization of Accreditation

The increased awareness of the need for quality assurance and/or accreditation has led to several new developments in accreditation, which have had both positive and negative aspects. Before discussing these developments, it is important to acknowledge the efforts of many countries to establish criteria and procedures for quality assurance recognition systems and approving accreditors. At the same time, it is necessary to recognize the increase in self-appointed and rather self-serving accreditors, as well as accreditation mills that sell bogus accreditation labels.

As higher education becomes increasingly subject to market forces, the profile, reputation and courses of a given institution or provider are more and more important. Institutions are making major investments in marketing and branding campaigns in order to gain name recognition and increase enrollments. Accreditation is part of the overall campaign and assures prospective students that the programs are of high standing. The desire for accreditation status is leading to the commercialization of quality assurance and accreditation, as programs and providers strive to gain as many accreditation "stars" as possible in order to increase competitiveness and perceived international legitimacy. Prospective students are challenged to distinguish between bona fide and rogue accreditors, especially when neither the cross-border provider nor the accreditor is nationally based or recognized as part of a national higher education system.

At the same time, networks of institutions and new organizations have appointed themselves as accreditors of their members. These are positive developments when seen through the lens of trying to improve the quality of their academic programs. But there is concern that they are not totally objective in their assessments and may be more interested in generating income than improving quality. While this can apply to both cross-border and domestic programs, it is particularly worrisome for cross-border programs, as attention to national policy objectives and cultural orientation is often neglected by foreign accreditors.

The growth of foreign degree mills (selling "parchment-only" degrees), accreditation mills (selling bogus accreditations for programs or institutions) and rogue for-profit providers (not recognized by national authorities) is a reality of which students, parents, employers, and the academic community now need to be aware (Garrett, 2005).

Who would have guessed two decades ago that international education would be struggling to deal with fake degrees and accreditations, that academic credentials would sometimes be earned but not recognized, and that non-regulated "fly-by-night" institutions would be blights on the international education scene? Of course, one must also acknowledge innovative developments by bona fide new providers and traditional universities that are delivering high quality programs and legitimate degrees through new types of arrangements and partnerships (franchise, twinning, double degree, and branch campus to name a few). The perpetual issue of balancing cost, quality and access calls into question the potential benefits and risks of cross-border education.

Double and Joint Degrees—Twice the Benefit or Double Counting?

Improvement in the quality of research, the teaching-learning process, and curriculum has long been heralded as a positive outcome of international collaboration. Higher education institutions have much to gain from internationalization through exchange of good practice, shared curricular reform, close research cooperation, and mobility of professors/students. Recently, joint programs have been established between institutions in different countries, leading to double or multiple degrees, and in some cases to joint degrees, although the latter face steeper legal constraints (European University Association, 2004). Joint programs are intended to provide a rich international and comparative academic experience for students and to improve their opportunities for employment (Kuder and Obst, 2009), but questionable adaptations and unintended consequences have also resulted. For instance, in some cases, double degrees can be nothing more than double-counting one set of course credits. In some cases, participating institutions have conferred two or even three credentials (one from each participating institution) for little more than the work load required for one degree.

While it may be very attractive for students to have two degrees from two institutions in two different countries, some might describe the situation as academic fraud if course requirements for two full degrees are not completed or if differentiated learning outcomes are not achieved (Knight, 2008c). It is important to add that there are many excellent and innovative joint and double degree programs being offered, especially by European institutions given the priority these programs have in the Bologna process (Schule, 2006). However, one of the unanticipated consequences has been the misuse or abuse of this new internationalization initiative. In cases where these programs span two or more jurisdictions, more work on the quality assurance and credential recognition is necessary because these programs can be exempt from national regulations.

Commodification and Commercialization: For-Profit Internationalization

Institutions overwhelmingly agree that internationalization brings benefits to higher education: 96 percent of responding institutions from 95 countries agreed with this assertion in the 2005 International Association of Universities (IAU) Internationalization Survey. Yet, this consensus is qualified by the fact that 70 percent also believe there are substantial risks associated with the international dimension of higher education (Knight, 2006a).

Overall, the number one risk identified in the survey was the commodification and commercialization of education programs. This consensus was widely shared among respondents from developing and developed countries. A regional-level analysis showed that four regions (Africa, Asia Pacific, Europe and North America) ranked commercialization as the top risk. In contrast, Latin America placed brain drain as number one and the Middle East ranked loss of cultural identity in first place.

The General Agreement on Trade in Services (GATS) has been a wake-up call for higher education around the world. Higher education has traditionally been seen as a "public good" and a "social responsibility" (Knight, 2008b). But with the advent of this new international trade agreement, higher education has become a tradable commodity, or more precisely in GATS terms, an internationally tradable service. Many see GATS as presenting new opportunities and benefits while others see it as introducing new risks. Others question why the trade sector needs to impose regulations at all, since the education sector has been using its own agreements and conventions for decades.

At the heart of the debate for many educators is the impact of increased commercial cross-border education on the purpose, role, and values of higher education. The growth in new commercial and private providers, the commodification of education, and the implications of new trade policy frameworks have stimulated serious reflection on the role, social commitment, and funding of public higher education institutions in society. The trinity of teaching, research, and service has traditionally guided the evolution of universities and their contribution to the social, cultural, human, scientific, and economic development of nations. Is the combination of these roles still valid, or can they now be disaggregated and rendered by different providers?

Finally, how will commercialization change the incentives for institutions to internationalize? Currently, one of the leading rationales at the institutional level for internationalization is that it makes graduates more internationally knowledgeable and interculturally skilled, and prepares them to live and work in more culturally diverse communities. Institutions must ask how an increased emphasis on the "buying and selling" of education across borders will affect the nature and priority given to academic, social and cultural rationales of non-profit international education activities (Altbach and Knight, 2007).

Cultural Diversity or Homogenization?

Debates on the impact of new forms of international academic mobility on cultural diversity often provoke strong positions and sentiments. Some take a positive view of the ways that modern information and communication technologies and the movement of people, ideas, and culture across national boundaries promote the fusion and hybridization of culture. Others contend that these same forces are eroding national cultural identities and leading to cultural homogenization, most often in the form of Westernization.

These arguments have often centered on education and its traditional role as a vehicle of acculturation, at times focusing on the specifics of curriculum content, language of instruction (particularly the increase in English) and the teaching-learning process in international education (Sehoole, 2008). Research has long focused on the impact of historic forms of colonization on education, but the place of internationalization in contemporary processes of cultural change has not been sufficiently studied.

Internationalization of higher education was originally conceived in terms of exchange and sharing of ideas, cultures, knowledge, and values. Formalized academic relations between countries were normally expressed in bilateral cultural and scientific agreements. Today, the agreements often must take trade, economic, and political factors into account, representing a significant shift from the original idea of academic exchange. Thus, there are two factors at play here: one is the potential for cultural homogenization, which may be perceived as threatening, and the second is the weakening of the cultural exchange component of internationalization in favor of relationships based more on economic and political concerns.

Status and Profile: World Rankings

There is no question that international and regional rankings of universities have become more popular and problematic in the last five years (Horn et al., 2007; Marginson and van der Wende, 2007). The heated debate about their validity, reliability and value continues. But at the same time, university presidents appear to use them to structure priorities, declaring in their strategic plans that a measurable outcome of internationalization will be the achievement of a specific position in one or more of the global ranking instruments. Some institutions perceive internationalization as a means to gain a worldwide profile and prestige. The intense competition for world rankings would have been impossible to imagine a mere 20 years ago, when international collaboration among universities, through academic exchanges and development cooperation projects, was the norm. Of course, these types of activities still take place, but the factors influencing internationalization are becoming increasingly complex, and the process is becoming increasingly competitive. Is international cooperation and exchange becoming overshadowed by competition for status, bright students, talented faculty, research grants, and membership in networks? The answer is probably yes, especially for those universities already placed in the top 25 percent of their national league tables or the two international ranking systems developed by Shanghai Jiao Tong University and Times Higher Education. Asia is one region of the world that takes competitiveness and rankings very seriously (Mok, 2007). National programs, such the 211 and 985 projects in China or the Brain Korea 21, aim to help their best research universities improve their international rankings (Kim and Nam, 2007; Liu, 2007).

The concept of "world-class universities" is a subject of intense scrutiny (Altbach and Balan, 2007), but "world-class" is still in the eye of the beholder, in spite of all the attention being given to rankings. National, regional, international and discipline/profession-specific rankings allow self-appointed ranking bodies, whether magazines, consumer guides, universities, newspapers or private companies, to make judgments about the "prestige" of universities of all types. But in spite of rhetoric about the "hollowness" of the ranking game, the competition among institutions hoping to be ranked as "world-class" is increasing, not diminishing.

Internationalization and the Knowledge Economy

The new reality is that universities play a central role in the new knowledge enterprise. Countries hoping to become regional education hubs or to develop education cities or knowledge villages see private education providers and branch campuses of foreign universities as key partners. While these initiatives include first-generation cross-border strategies like branch campuses and franchised programs, they also include projects of another magnitude such as co-locating a critical mass of foreign universities with private companies, research and development enterprises, and science and technology parks to collectively support and develop new knowledge industries. The emergence of education hubs and cities is concrete proof that higher education is gaining more importance and influence as an economic and political actor in the burgeoning knowledge era—but at what cost?

International education cities and regional education hubs represent new territory for the higher education sector. That being said, it is important to recognize that the higher education sector is not always the sponsor of these new education initiatives.

In many cases, branch campuses of foreign institutions are seen as tenants in huge multifaceted complexes just like any other commercial enterprise. Economic development boards, tourism authorities, science and technology parks, and multinational investment companies see higher education institutions and providers as key players in the preparation of future knowledge workers and the production of new knowledge. No matter how distasteful many academics will find the treatment of education as a commodity, the development of these hubs and education cities is positive proof that education is seen as a commodity to be used for developing the required human capital to gain a competitive advantage in the knowledge economy.

What Next?

These developments and unintended consequences illustrate that it is necessary to stay alert to unexpected twists and turns along the road to internationalization, since nothing unfolds entirely as expected. With innovation comes new opportunities, successes and threats. It is imperative that the international, intercultural and global dimensions of higher education continue to be proactive, responsive and innovative while keeping a close watch on unanticipated implications. As internationalization matures and grows, a critical eye and strong will are needed to monitor intended and unintended results so that benefits to individuals, institutions, nations and society are maximized and risks minimized for this year and 25 years hence.

REFERENCES

Agarwal, P., Said, M., Sehoole C., Sirozie, M., & De Wit, H. (2007). The dynamics of international student circulation in a global context. In Altbach, P., & Mc Gill Peterson, P. (Eds.), *Higher education in the new century, global challenges and innovative ideas* (109-144). Rotterdam: Sense Publishers.

Altbach, P., & Balan, J. (Eds) (2007). *World class worldwide: Transforming research universities in Asia and Latin America*. Baltimore: The Johns Hopkins University Press.

Altbach, P., and Knight, J. (2007). The internationalization of higher education: Motivations and realities. *Journal of Studies In International Education, 11:3/4*, 290-305.

Bohm A., Davis, D. Meares D., & Pearce D. (2002). *The global student mobility 2025 report: Forecasts of the global demand for international education*. Canberra, Australia: IDP.

European University Association. (2004). *Developing joint masters programmes for Europe*. Brussels, Belgium: EUA.

Garrett, R. (2005). *Fraudulent, sub-standard, ambiguous: The alternative borderless higher education*. Briefing Note - July 2005. London: Observatory on Borderless Higher Education.

Horn, A., Hendel, D., & Fry, G. (2007). Ranking the international dimension of top research universities in the United States. *Journal of Studies in International Education, 11:3/4*, 330-358.

Kim, K.S., & Nam, S. (2007). The making of a world-class university at the periphery: Seoul National University. In Altbach, P., & Balan, J. (Eds.), *World class worldwide: Transforming research universities in Asia and Latin America*. Baltimore (pp. 122-142). The Johns Hopkins University Press.

Kuder, M., & Obst, D. (2009). *Joint and double degree programs in the transatlantic context: A survey report*. New

York: Institute of International Education and Freie Universität Berlin.

Knight, J. (2008a). *Higher education in turmoil: The changing world of internationalization*. Rotterdam: Sense Publisher.

Knight, J. (2008b). The role of cross-border education in the debate on education as a public good and private commodity. *Journal of Asian Public Policy, 1:2*, 174-188.

Knight, J. (2008c). *Double and joint degrees: Vexing questions and issues*. London: Observatory on Borderless Higher Education.

Knight, J. (2007). Cross-border tertiary education: An introduction. In *Cross-border tertiary education: A way towards capacity development*. OECD, World Bank and NUFFIC. Paris, France pp. 21-46.

Knight, J. (2006a). *Internationalization of higher education: New directions, new challenges. 2005 IAU global survey report*. Paris: International Association of Universities.

Knight, J. (2006b). *Higher education crossing borders: A guide to the implications of GATS for cross-border education*. Paris: Commonwealth of Learning and UNESCO.

Knight, J. (2004). Internationalization remodeled: Rationales, strategies and approaches. *Journal for Studies in International Education, 8:1*, 5-31.

Liu, N. (2007). Research universities in China: Differentiation, classification and future world-class status. In Altbach, P., & Balan, J. (Eds.), *World class worldwide: Transforming research universities in Asia and Latin America* (pp. 54-70). Baltimore: The Johns Hopkins University Press.

Marginson, S. & van der Wende, M. (2007). To rank or to be ranked: The impact of global rankings in higher education. *Journal of Studies in International Education, 11:3/4*, 306-329.

Ministry of Trade and Industry. (2003). *Growing our economy*. Singapore Government. Retrieved February 20, 2009, from http://app.mti.gov.sg/data/pages/507/doc/DSE_recommend.pdf

Mok, K. H. (2007). Questing for internationalization of universities in Asia: Critical reflections. *Journal of Studies in International Education, 11(3-4)*, 433-454.

Schule, U. (2006). Joint and double degrees within the European Higher Education Area: Towards further internationalization of business degrees. *Papers on International Business Education*. Paris: Consortium of International Double Degrees.

Sehoole, C. (2008). Issues, policies, and developments of internationalization in Africa: Comparative analysis. In Teferra, D., & Knight, J. (Eds.), *Higher education in Africa: The international dimension* (pp. 394-407). Boston, MA: Center for International Higher Education and African Association of Universities.

Vincent-Lancrin, S. (2004). Implications of recent developments for access and equity, cost and funding, quality and capacity building. In *Internationalisation and Trade in Higher Education* (pp. 237-296). Paris: CERI/OECD.

About the Contributors

Rajika Bhandari is the Director of Research and Evaluation at the Institute of International Education (IIE), where she leads two major research projects—*Open Doors* and *Project Atlas*—that measure international higher education mobility at the domestic (U.S.) and international level. She also conducts evaluations of IIE's international scholarship and fellowship programs. Before joining IIE, Dr. Bhandari was a Senior Researcher at MPR Associates, an educational research firm in Berkeley, California, that provides research and evaluation services to the U.S. Department of Education, state departments of education, and foundations. She also served as the Assistant Director for Evaluation at the Mathematics and Science Education Network at the University of North Carolina at Chapel Hill, where she directed research and evaluations of mathematics and science education pre-college and professional development programs. She holds a PhD in Psychology from North Carolina State University and a BA (Honors) in Psychology from the University of Delhi, India.

Peggy Blumenthal is Executive Vice President and Chief Operating Officer at the Institute of International Education. Responsible for the overall programmatic and administrative operations of IIE, Ms. Blumenthal also directly supervises IIE's research activities, corporate- and foundation-funded scholarships and training activities such as the Global Engineering Educational Exchange. The Institute of International Education, a private nonprofit organization with 600 staff members and 33 offices and representatives around the globe, is a world leader in academic exchange and the development of globally competent professionals and future leaders. Ms. Blumenthal holds a BA from Harvard University in Modern Chinese History and an MA in American Studies from the University of Hawaii at Manoa.

Titus Galama is a management scientist at the RAND Corporation. He holds an MSc in physics (cum laude, 1995) and a PhD in astrophysics (cum laude, 1999) from the University of Amsterdam, the Netherlands. After completion of his thesis, he worked as a Fairchild Postdoctoral Prize Fellow at Caltech, Pasadena. He is the author of more than 50 articles on astrophysics published in scientific journals. Following his career in astrophysics, he earned an MBA from INSEAD and worked as a senior strategy consultant for a global strategy consulting firm on a variety of projects in health care and biotechnology for companies ranging from mature start-ups to global conglomerates. His current policy research interests are in education; science, technology, and innovation; and the economics of health and retirement. His recent research concerns U.S. competitiveness in science and technology and the U.S. science and engineering workforce.

Ellen Hazelkorn is the Director of Research and Enterprise, and Dean of the Graduate Research School, Dublin Institute of Technology, Ireland; she also leads the Higher Education Policy Research Unit. She is a consultant to the OECD Programme on Institutional Management of Higher Education (IMHE) and is also associated with the International Association of Universities (IAU). Professor Hazelkorn is Rapporteur for the EU Expert Group on Assessment of University-based Research and a member of National Digital Research Centre (NDRC) Management Board; the Arts, Humanities and Social Sciences Foresight Working Group; and the International Advisory Council of the Irish Research Council for the Humanities and Social Sciences. She is a member of the Executive Committee of the Dean and European Academic Network (DEAN) and the Editorial Boards of *Higher Education Management and Policy* (OECD) and *Higher Education Policy* (IAU). She is leading an international study on the *Impact and Influence of Rankings on Higher Education Decision-Making and Academic Behaviour* (www.oecd.org/edu/imhe/rankings). *How Rankings Are Reshaping Higher Education: The Competition for World-Class Excellence Goes Global* is forthcoming in late 2009.

James Hosek's recent work has been on U.S. competitiveness in science and technology and the U.S. science and engineering workforce. He directs the Forces and Resources Policy Center of the National Defense Research Institute at RAND, and he has published studies in defense manpower on a wide range of topics in the areas of personnel supply, compensation and quality; and in labor economics on unemployment, labor supply and migration. Hosek is Editor-in-Chief of *The RAND Journal of Economics*, a leading journal on industrial organization, regulation, and contracts, and he is Professor of Economics at the Pardee RAND Graduate School. He has served as RAND Corporate Research Manager in Human Capital and Chair of the Economics and Statistics Department. He holds a BA in English from Cornell University and MA and PhD degrees in economics from the University of Chicago.

Jane Knight focuses her research and professional interests on the international dimension of higher education at the institutional, system, national, and international levels. Her work in over 60 countries helps to bring a comparative, development and international policy perspective to her research, teaching and policy work. Dr. Knight is the author/editor of many publications on internationalization concepts and strategies, quality assurance, institutional management, mobility, cross-border education, trade and capacity building. Her latest 2008 publications include *Higher Education in Turmoil: The Changing World of Internationalization* (author), *Financing Access and Equity in Higher Education* (editor), and *Higher Education in Africa: The International Dimension* (co-editor). She is an Adjunct Professor at Ontario Institute for Studies in Education, University of Toronto, and was a Fulbright New Century Scholar for 2007-2008.

Ulla Kriebernegg studied English and American studies and German philology at Karl-Franzens University Graz, Austria, and at University College Dublin, Ireland. She was also a Visiting Scholar at the Boston College Center for International Higher Education (CIHE). From 1999-2007, Kriebernegg worked for Graz University's Office of International Relations, where she was centrally involved in joint degree development. She now works as an Assistant Professor for the Center for the Study of the Americas at Karl-Franzens University Graz, Austria. Her doctoral research explores the impact of the Bologna reforms on U.S. higher education ("Transatlantic Relationships in Higher Education: An Analysis of Cultural Narratives"). Her research interests are inter-American studies, interculturality, and U.S. and European higher education policy.

Shepherd Laughlin is Program Coordinator with the Membership and Higher Education Services division at IIE's New York headquarters. Since joining IIE, he has edited several publications related to educational mobility, including two IIE White Papers and the first title in the Global Education Research Reports series, *U.S.-China Educational Exchange: Perspectives on a Growing Partnership*. His senior thesis, *Global China, Local Chinas: Modernization and Ethnic Identity in the People's Republic*, was selected for publication in 2007 by the Brown University Senior Honors Thesis Publication Competition. In 2005, Mr. Laughlin traveled to Beijing on a Freeman-ASIA scholarship to study Mandarin, and he later spent time in France studying at Sciences-Po. He holds an A.B. in International Relations from Brown University.

Roberta Maierhofer is Professor at the Department of American Studies of the University of Graz, Austria, and Adjunct Professor at Binghamton University, New York. Since joining the staff of the Department of American Studies in 1998, she has played an instrumental role in the university's international study, joint study and exchange programs, as well as the development of its Office for International Relations. She was elected Vice Rector for International Relations in 1999 and then appointed for another period as Vice Rector for International Relations and Affirmative Action for Women under the new Austrian University Act in 2003. Since 2004, she has served as Vice Rector for International Relations and Interdisciplinary Cooperation, and since 2007 she has been academic director of the newly founded Center for the Study of the Americas of the University of Graz. Her research focuses on American literature and cultural studies, feminist literature and research, transatlantic cooperation in education, and aging studies.

Sabine O'Hara began her tenure as Vice President of IIE and Executive Director of the Council for International Exchange of Scholars in July 2007. A respected author and researcher, she is well known for her expertise in sustainable economic development and global education. She has lectured around the globe; is the author of two books and numerous articles, book chapters and research reports; and has developed and taught undergraduate and graduate courses on topics like sustainable economic development, economics and ethics, cultural perspectives on valuation, stakeholder processes and discourse. Before joining IIE/CIES, Dr. O'Hara was the 10th president of Roanoke College and held faculty and administrative positions at Concordia College Moorhead, Green Mountain College, and Rensselaer Polytechnic Institute. She was a visiting scholar at Harvard University. Dr. O'Hara serves on the board of directors of several national and international organizations, including the Association for Social Economics, and is President of the United States Society for Ecological Economics. She is a native of Germany and received a PhD in environmental economics from the University of Göttingen.

N. V. Varghese is currently Head of Governance and Management in Education at the International Institute for Educational Planning (IIEP/UNESCO), Paris. He was a Professor and Head of Educational Planning at the National Institute of Educational Planning and Administration (NIEPA), New Delhi. While at NIEPA, he was also responsible for the Asian Network of Training and Research Institutions in Educational Planning (ANTRIEP) and was editor of its newsletter. He was Head of the Training and Education Programmes Unit of IIEP from 2001 to 2006. He assumed the responsibilities as Head of Higher Education and Specialized Training in September 2006 and as Head of Governance and Management in Education in January 2008. He has published books and articles in the areas of educational planning, financing and quality of education. His recent publications include *Impact of the economic crisis on higher education in East Asia* (2001), *Growth and expansion of private higher education in Africa* (2006), *GATS and higher education* (2007), and *Globalization of higher education and cross-border student mobility* (2008).

Bernd Wächter is the Director of the Academic Cooperation Association (ACA), a consortium of European and global agencies. ACA is a think-tank that promotes innovation and internationalization in higher education. In his first post, at the University of Kassel (Germany), he developed international degree programs; he then joined the British Council before becoming the Director of International Affairs at the Fachhochschule Darmstadt. He later became the head of the European section of the German Academic Exchange Service (DAAD), then Director of Higher Education in the Brussels Socrates Office, with overall administrative responsibility for the Erasmus program in Europe. In 1998, he took up his post as the Director of ACA. Wächter has published widely on internationalization in higher education and is the editor of the *ACA Papers on International Cooperation in Higher Education*. Wächter studied at the universities of Hull (UK), Giessen and Marburg (Germany). He lives in Brussels and is married to Thora Magnusdottir, a lovely lady from Iceland.